MW00424959

Cape Cod
LIBRARIES

Cape Cod

LIBRARIES

A HISTORY AND GUIDE

Gerree Q. Hogan

THE
History
PRESS

Published by The History Press
Charleston, SC
www.historypress.com

First published 2023

Manufactured in the United States

ISBN 9781467152655

Library of Congress Control Number: 2022950047

To my wife, Teri J. Pierce, who makes me laugh every single day, and to my sister, Charlene M. Hogan, EdD, who took me to our hometown (Ashland, Massachusetts) library in a little red wagon—and taught me to read.

CONTENTS

CONTENTS

Cape Cod Libraries

A map of Cape Cod Libraries. *Teri J. Pierce.*

PREFACE

*L*ibraries are seductive: the enticing abundance of books, the peaceful hush, the golden dust dancing in slanting sunlight, the creaking wood floors—all free, all for everyone, all the time.

Only two types of responses greeted my news that I was writing a book about Cape Cod libraries. One was raised eyebrows, a pause and an excited, "Oh, that's great!" The other was raised eyebrows, a pause and a pitying, "Oh, that's…great."

Needless to say, you and I belong to the first group. We already know how amazing libraries are, how they are filled with everything wonderful that can possibly exist on paper, CD, DVD, microfilm and microchip, plus people who genuinely want to help us find it. We realize the almost unbelievable fact that everything in the library is free for us to use, and if you don't find what you're looking for in one library, you can look for it in another one—also at no cost. The librarians in that other library will move heaven and earth to assist in your search as well. Happily, this process can go on and on to infinity. And it's all free!

People in the small second group would nod kindly (if somewhat sadly) at me as I told them that on Cape Cod alone there are thirty-four libraries, unaware how staggering a statistic I had just imparted. (Hampden County, also in Massachusetts, has thirty-five libraries but double the population of our Barnstable County.)

Or are the pitiers still stuck in the ancient stereotype that library lovers are conservative, reverent and fusty? (I am the very opposite.) They edge away from the conversation, tell me good luck with the project and relegate me to the dusty stacks of "old lady writing a book that no one would ever read, let alone publish."

Well! Here we are. What fun to write a book that my fellow library lovers can appreciate. To those who are reading this only because they love Cape Cod, welcome—you are about to embark on a library adventure, too, because I challenge anyone to not want to visit a library on this peninsula after learning a little about their history, seeing how the building has changed, looking at their insides and marveling at what fills them besides books to borrow. (Think telescopes, toys, laptops, tablets, scanners, printers and puzzles.) Did I mention that all this is free?

When I moved to Cape Cod in the 1980s, I was awed by the number of libraries here. I expected fifteen—one per town—but there are thirty-four: seven in the town of Barnstable, five in Dennis, five in Falmouth, three each in Harwich and Yarmouth and two in Chatham, plus one in each of the nine remaining towns. In the process of doggedly "learning the back roads," a goal toward which all year-rounders strive in order to survive the summer traffic, I discovered many libraries, big and small, pretty and utilitarian, but not one just ordinary. Nothing, no, *nothing*, is ordinary about Cape Cod.

Many a time I followed a book quest to another town's library and stood ogling the building for a while, enchanted by its unique charm. Woods Hole was one of these, with its rocky exterior; Eldredge Library in Chatham was another, a Gothicky castle in the center of town. But it was the sweet little South Dennis Free Public Library, a Victorian dollhouse hidden in a thicket, that made me fairly swoon with delight—and the determination that, once and for all, I just had to write a book about Cape Cod libraries.

After all, I had been inside every library on Cape Cod, right? I was therefore uniquely qualified to learn a bit more about their individual history, take pictures and enlighten the rest of the world on the spectacular quantity and quality of our library love. So I set about an accounting. Meaning, I counted them. That is when I had a reality seizure.

There were more libraries on the official list than I had actually visited. I had missed a few. In thirty-five years of living on Cape Cod, I genuinely believed I had seen each one. There was no time to waste. I zoomed out to East Dennis, wended my way through narrow lanes to Quivet Neck and came upon—there's no other expression for it—the secret Jacob Sears Library in all its chateau-like magnificence. How, how had I never heard of this magical place? Could this mean that there might be more hidden libraries on my favorite peninsula? Noooo. Yes. Several more.

Add the tiny Harwich Port Library, the even tinier Chase Library in West Harwich and the teeny-tiny South Chatham Library, and I can finally and unequivocally state that I am well acquainted with all thirty-four wonderful Cape Cod libraries. Whew. However, there turned out to be a few whose recent renovations rendered them so shockingly different as to be completely new to me; Eastham is one. I was speechless at its beautiful beyond belief transformation. Bright red furniture in a library! Provincetown somehow grew a ship in its insides since the last time I visited—the library, anyway. Mashpee is a fantastic, updated version of itself compared to its 1990s self.

So, instead of merely intending to write a book about them one day, I decided to start. It was early 2020. Yes, you're ahead of me; I got thwarted. The coronavirus pandemic closed all my libraries in one disheartening fell swoop and kept them closed for many months. I languished. The librarians were valiantly keeping the flow of books going by way of "curbside pickup," which helped my reading addiction but did nothing to ease my symptoms of library building withdrawal. I pined for the aromas of book dust and beeswaxed floorboards and new book ink.

When the COVID-19 laws began to loosen up slightly, we were finally granted fifteen masked minutes inside a library with strict instructions to stay six feet away from other patrons. I had tears in my eyes, I admit it, when I slipped into the West Yarmouth Library and breathed in that heady mixture of old paper and old wood: this place is an old friend. It was so good to be home.

We each learned things from the pandemic. "Don't postpone joy" was tattooed on my heart once and for all. I made a list of every town's libraries and began to formulate a format for this book. Alphabetical? By size? My favorites, ranked? No. I decided to use the geographical labels that Cape Codders use—Upper Cape, Mid-Cape, Lower Cape and Outer Cape.

Now to find a publisher. I had often been drawn to a series of trade paperbacks with sepia-toned photographs on the cover. They were usually about one town or a local industry. I typed "sepia-toned cover" into Google and Arcadia Publishing popped up, then the "contact us" page, and within days I was preparing a New Author's Proposal for *Cape Cod Libraries*. Three weeks later, my book was given the go-ahead by the nice people at Arcadia, although with its more appropriate imprint The History Press, and after a few more months of my researching, writing and photographing, it was published and printed and here you are holding it.

I am joyful. It is soul satisfying to gift this shortcut to fellow library lovers: a compendium of our favorite buildings on gorgeous Cape Cod.

Why is it so important to memorialize thirty-four buildings full of books on one peninsula in Massachusetts? Because Cape Cod is so much more than beaches and souvenirs. Our libraries endure—by changing to include innovative technologies while buildings and values remain the same to satisfy our fundamental need for constancy. They endure because every shelf holds vast knowledge and entertainment, and it's all free. And because Cape Cod libraries smell so good with that extra tang of salt from the sea.

Gerree Quinn Hogan
Hyannis, Massachusetts
March 2022

ACKNOWLEDGEMENTS

*L*ibrarians love libraries too, and most of them were extraordinarily helpful in helping me find information and photographs for this book.

Deb Rich, the director of the Sandwich Town Archives, gave me much attention and compassion during my first foray into looking for "any old photos you might have," teaching me some lingo and technical things along the way.

Rebekah Ambrose-Dalton, the archivist in the William B. Nickerson Collection at Cape Cod Community College, tirelessly searched for, found and scanned scores of pictures for me.

Kristin MacLeod, director of Nevins Library in Methuen, Massachusetts, a library exactly one hundred miles from my office on Cape Cod, allowed me to use her library's collection of archival Cape library images without hesitation.

My wife, Teri J. Pierce, created the map of Cape Cod libraries for this book.

My sister, Charlene M. Hogan, and our cousin, Susan Willis Davis, gave me the beautiful images of Provincetown Public Library.

My editors at The History Press, Michael G. Kinsella and Abigail Fleming, deserve praise for being good-natured and encouraging.

LAND ACKNOWLEDGEMENT

The land on which every Cape Cod Library was built is the traditional unceded territory of the People of the First Light: The Wampanoag Nation.

I acknowledge the painful history of genocide, forced occupation and taking of their territory, and I honor and respect the many diverse Indigenous people connected to this land from time immemorial.

INTRODUCTION

Few things annoy a self-proclaimed logical researcher more than having to use old data, but the coronavirus pandemic that began in 2020 permanently scarred and skewed every library statistic during the time of quarantines, shutdowns, mandatory mask wearing, infectious variants spiking and curbside book pickups. I had to resort to using 2019 data in this 2022 book, which irks me no end but makes perfect sense in a nonsensical pandemic world. The data are not actually outdated, for they represent an accurate, library-by-library comparison of what we, one and all, used to take for granted: that happy, regular life would go on as usual and nothing would ever cause public libraries to close their doors to us. Even though the actual shuttering was temporary, we library lovers will bear the marks of the torment for a long time to come.

Lesson learned: never take anything for granted. Enjoy every minute you have, and if you can't manage that today, double up on enjoyment tomorrow. Plan fun, learn everything and don't postpone joy. It's later than you think.

A word about the interconnectedness of Cape Cod libraries: almost all of them are—through CLAMS. That's Cape Libraries Automated Materials Sharing, which can be accessed online at www.clamsnet.org. Of the thirty-four libraries described herein, the only ones *not* part of the CLAMS network are South Chatham Public Library, Harwich Port Library and Chase Library in West Harwich—all three because they don't have computers—and Sandwich Public Library because it bravely chose to align instead with Old Colony Library Network in 2004 (www.ocln.org). Though the decision was met with disappointment by some Cape Cod libraries—long accustomed to enjoying extreme peninsular loyalty—in practicality the change gave all residents of Barnstable County access to the contents of twenty-seven *more* libraries in southeastern Massachusetts, from Quincy to Plymouth. OCLN will gladly ship a book from any member library to Sandwich, where Cape Codders can easily go pick it up. It's a valuable benefit. Some true library lovers might prefer to drive off Cape to those OCLN towns to retrieve a book themselves, if only as an excuse to go discover a new library building.

You might notice in reading this book that there was a flurry of library building activity in the 1890s. It's no coincidence, though civic pride and intercommunity competition might also account for the sudden increase in the number of libraries being built. It was the Free Public Library Movement finally making its inexorable way from Boston to Cape Cod; what started in earnest during the early 1800s culminated in 1848 when the Massachusetts General Court allowed the City of Boston to establish a library that would be free to all. By 1858, the Boston Public Library had been completed on Boylston Street as the city's first "purpose-built" library.

The vision of free libraries was to make books available for every person, regardless of socioeconomic status. The first libraries in the United States, as well as abroad, were private colections of books in private homes, usually only for the well-to-do. Next came subscription libraries, also for those with plenty of money plus leisure time to read; members paid annual dues along with a fee per book borrowed. These types of libraries, therefore, were not in the spirit of a democratic society, and when enough people realized that a better-educated population improved life for everyone, free libraries were made possible by legislation to spend public money on creating them.

By 1880, almost half the towns and cities in Massachusetts had a free library; ten years later, the Free Public Library Commission of Massachusetts was established by "An Act to Promote the Establishment and Efficiency of Free Public Libraries [Acts of 1890, chapter 347]." This helped communities establish libraries—and give them one hundred dollars seed money for books. All at once there was a building boom; most public libraries were supported by the town, others were privately funded and the rest were a hybrid of private with some municipal support.

Though there are no Carnegie libraries on Cape Cod, many of ours were constructed with funds donated in a similar fashion. Andrew Carnegie (1835–1919) was a steel magnate who gave millions to build libraries in more than 1,600 American cities and towns between 1886 and 1919. My own hometown library in Ashland, Massachusetts, is a Carnegie library, and when

I was a child, I thought it unrivaled for sheer beauty and magical powers. On the Cape, we had our own Andrew Carnegies: Emily Howland Bourne in Bourne, the Westons in Sandwich, William Sturgis in Barnstable Village, Martha Lee Whelden in West Barnstable, Caleb Chase in West Harwich, Henry Brooks in Harwich, Marcellus Eldredge in Chatham and the list goes on. Perhaps just as important are the contributions of regular people; "The Friends of" each library who work at fundraising to furnish new technologies (as well as instruction for the less tech-savvy), extra children's programs and book clubs to draw teenagers' interest.

Now, I love the internet. I love every single good thing about it. Answers to almost any question in a split second, any time of the day or night—amazing. But libraries are community; they hold the best of what has been learned since the dawn of time, under one roof, together with the dust of ages and a century of wood polish and other people milling about browsing contentedly. Internet be damned—libraries *must* go on.

Librarians are the guardians who can't wait to let you in. Revere them. Many times during the process of researching and writing this book I have been moved by the amazing dedication of all the librarians in all the towns in all the past decades—and I have trembled with the responsibility of writing about their libraries. I have wondered what they might think of me, a non-librarian from a future century, having the audacity to tell everyone what I have managed to dig up (about some) or report on (the rest).

I have told the truth, regardless.

PART I

The Upper Cape

I

SANDWICH

SANDWICH PUBLIC LIBRARY
142 MAIN STREET, SANDWICH, MA 02563
508-888-0625
WWW.SANDWICHPUBLICLIBRARY.COM

When I got my library card, that's when my life began.
—Rita Mae Brown (b. 1944, American feminist writer)

At once anachronistic and futuristic, Sandwich has steadfastly maintained its charm while providing the latest technology for its residents. There are no lit-from-inside signs in the whole town—certainly no neon. The duck pond has a working gristmill with a paddle wheel. Free, delicious drinking water runs day and night next to Town Hall; take as much as you like (gallons, if you want), anytime. These are the old-fashioned things about the oldest incorporated town on Cape Cod.

The Sandwich Library of the twenty-first century, however, is entirely up-to-date and state of the art. Humble beginnings transitioned into grand progress without losing any inherent dignity, and the librarians aren't totalitarian.

The rules were strict in 1891 when the first Board of Library Trustees met to decide how the Free Public Library of Sandwich would function. Patrons had to be at least twelve and could take out only one book per person (two per household) at a time. Fines for overdue books were two cents per day; this price stayed the same until 2021, when book fines were abolished altogether.

Some things never change: too eager to wait until she gets home, she reads on the library steps in 1911. *Sandwich Town Archives.*

On May 19, 1891, the *Sandwich Observer* announced:

> *The State's gift of 175 volumes to the Sandwich Public Library have arrived and are now in the possession of the trustees. The opening of the Library to the public will probably take place very shortly.*

In February 1892, the *Observer* observed,

> *Seven hundred volumes are now the property of the Sandwich Public Library. This is surely a good beginning. New quarters will soon be an imperative necessity.*

Space in the lower floor of Sandwich Town Hall was created, and with donations from events like a baseball game played by the town's tradesmen against its professional men (that netted $13) and a night of entertainment by Joseph Jefferson reminiscing about his early years on the stage ($400), the library boasted more than 1,600 books. Rules were relaxed slightly in 1896 so that patrons could take out two books, but only one of them could be fiction. Ten years later, the librarian was earning $150 per year, and an even bigger building was needed. The list of benefactors reads like a street index of Sandwich: Nye, Faunce, Chipman, Dillingham, Howland, Carleton, Wing, Hoxie, plus many more.

William H.H. and Sophia Weston, natives of Sandwich from glassmaking families, bequeathed the staggering sum of $45,000 for a brand-new library; the Weston Memorial Library was completed in 1910 with enough shelves for 10,000 books. (The count at the time was 3,300, but they were thinking ahead—could they ever have imagined well over 110,000 materials 100 years later?)

The new building, an excellent example of Edwardian Beaux-Arts architecture, was opened to the public on 1-11-11 (that's *1911*, of course). Over the next few years, the librarian's salary was raised to $400 per year, and the building was open several days each week. In 1913, the trustees voted that "when the power of electricity comes into town we put it into the library," which occurred in 1914. It cost $400. At the same time, it was decreed that a decorating company would spruce up the library in honor of the town's 275th anniversary of incorporation; the spending limit in this instance was $5.

Five decades later, the book collection had grown beyond shelf capacity. Two momentous bequests in the 1960s allowed the library to add much-needed space. Artist Dodge MacKnight willed $250,000, and former trustee Mary Crocker Baker bequeathed $100,000, so new wings were added in their names.

After additional redesigns and now triple the original floor space, its grounds have evolved as well. A handsome, open book–shaped stone bench along the brick walkway to Sandwich Library reads:

> *"Tell me, what is it you plan to do with your one wild and precious life?" from "The Summer Day" by Mary Oliver, Pulitzer Prize winning poet and longtime resident of Cape Cod. Presented with deep appreciation to the Sandwich Public Library for continuing to enrich the literary life of our community. Titcomb's Bookshop, 2017.*

Nearby is the artists' chiseled byline: "Created by Dave Campbell and Michael Magyar, Celebrating 50 years of Titcomb's Bookshop." (Where else but Cape Cod is there such a devoted friendship between a library and a bookstore just down the road?)

Dignified lanterns on tall posts dot the pretty landscaping around the library. There's a winsome stone cherub in the garden at the front door, too, that is always reading a book and sometimes wearing a lost-and-found mitten or hat.

A 2020 "space reallocation" transformed the layout. Its previous 1980s décor was industrialist fun, but the new configuration is exquisite

Funky chairs in shades of blue create ambience in Sandwich Public Library. *Author's collection.*

in practicality and ambiance. The footprint is identical; that's where the similarity ends. There's a long Tech Bar with tall stools and every sort of electronic outlet anyone would need, and numerous computer stations make researching easier. The Children's Room was moved across the building to be near the elevator and restrooms (brilliant). All the kids love the low porthole to see what's going on in the rest of the library, and there are comfortable sofas and chairs in which to read or play.

The Sandwich Town Archives have taken over the former children's area, so there's enough space to fit all the unique reference books and materials for this town, which was named for Sandwich in Kent, England, not for the Earl of Sandwich (who wasn't inventing lunch menus until almost one hundred years after the Cape Cod town was colonized). Specialized climate control protects the valuable information here for future researchers.

The library has some museum passes that no other Cape Cod library has. The pass for Buttonwood Park Zoo in New Bedford allows four people admission at no charge. The Sandwich Glass Museum is free for two people. All the rest offer varying discounts and are well worth it: Boston Children's Museum; Cahoon Museum of American Art in Cotuit; Cape Cod Museum of Art in Dennis; Isabella Stewart Gardner Museum, Boston; John F. Kennedy Library & Museum in Boston; Museum of Fine Arts, Boston; Museum of Science in Boston; Mystic Seaport in Mystic, Connecticut; the New Bedford Whaling Museum; New England Aquarium in Boston; and the Whydah Pirate Museum in West Yarmouth.

Seating groups and the delightfully named "collaborative areas" give a nod to mid-century modern design, both beautiful and substantial. Muted blue tones in the furnishings and carpet make this library feel calm, even hushed, without being silent.

2

BOURNE

Jonathan Bourne Public Library
19 Sandwich Road, Bourne, MA 02532
508-759-0600
www.BourneLibrary.org

The library is an arena of possibility,
opening both a window into the soul and a door onto the world.
—Rita Dove (b. 1952, American poet)

When Emily Howland Bourne chose the site for a public library to further memorialize her father in 1897 (he already had a whole town named for him, and she kept finding things that could bear his name even after she'd be dead), she decided on the banks of the Manomet River, within view of the house in which her father had been born and lived until he was seventeen.

That house was later destroyed (and the river incorporated into the Atlantic) by the dredging of the Cape Cod Canal in 1913, but the English Renaissance architecture of the original library remains as the Jonathan Bourne Historical Center, 30 Keene Street. Boston architect Henry Vaughn designed it, featuring yellow tapestry brick, a red slate roof and Palladian windows. There's even a stained-glass window of St. Michael and the Dragon in the reading room. The present Jonathan Bourne Public Library luxuriates in its roomy converted school just around the corner on Sandwich Road.

The Jonathan Bourne Library serves a population of twenty thousand from Bourne's ten villages. *Author's collection.*

Jonathan Bourne sought his fortune on ships out of New Bedford in 1828 while still a teenager, and eventually he sailed into success as a whaling merchant. By 1884, he was a state legislator who helped the western section of Sandwich separate into its own town; the grateful leaders of the project named the new town after him.

Bourne is a sprawling and diverse place, with a mammoth military base and a National Cemetery, plus two iconic bridges connecting the Cape and the mainland. As the first landfall after the Cape Cod Canal—whether you travel over the Sagamore Bridge or the Bourne Bridge—all the delightful little villages for which the peninsula is famous become obvious fast: Buzzards Bay, Bournedale, Sagamore, Sagamore Beach, Gray Gables, Monument Beach, Pocasset, Cataumet, Joint Base Cape Cod (military) and Bourne Village.

Only one library serves the civilian population of 20,000 in all these villages: the Jonathan Bourne Public Library, housed since 1985 in the former Frances Stowell Grammar School. It has a collection of more than 60,000 materials and a circulation of 172,000 in a typical year. While several other Cape Cod towns have a library for each village, this one does the work of ten. The staff members keep up with the demand, and they manage to make everyone feel welcome here.

Programs for children include Babies & Books; Toddler Hop, Skip, and Read; and Science Saturdays. For adults, there are book discussion groups, appointments for technology help and free notary public service. Museum passes for free or discounted admission are available to Boston Children's Museum; Buttonwood Park Zoo, New Bedford; Cape Cod Children's Museum, Mashpee; Cape Cod Museum of Art, Dennis; Heritage Museum and Gardens, Sandwich; Historic New England, Haverhill; Isabella Stewart Gardner Museum, Boston; Museum of Fine Arts, Boston; New Bedford Whaling Museum; New England Aquarium, Boston; Plimoth Patuxet & the Mayflower, Plymouth; Robbins Museum of Archaeology, Middleboro; Sandwich Glass Museum; USS Constitution Museum, Charlestown; and the Whydah Pirate Museum, West Yarmouth.

Emily Howland Bourne, by all accounts quite a character for the times in which she lived (1835–1922), had so much personal integrity and compassion for the underserved that her relatives contested her will on the grounds that she was insane. The document was perfectly clear about the intention of her bequests:

> As the property of my father was sufficient to amply provide for his children, it has accordingly seemed right to me not to add to the large fortunes of those who are most nearly related to me, but rather to do what I think they would most appreciate, and, after making them gifts as tokens of my affection, to devote the bulk of my fortune to trying to make comfortable the lives of those who have slender means and to the relief of the needy and suffering poor and the general benefit of humanity.

It turned out that one relative, her niece, did not appreciate receiving only $10,000 out of Bourne's $1 million estate, so she spent several years waging war in New York courts.

The philanthropist's idiosyncrasies, such as sleeping wrapped up in flannel like a mummy, were held up for public scrutiny as being as crazy as those of her mother (Jonathan's wife), who had a mental illness. Even a young nurse to whom Emily Bourne had given an automobile was compelled to testify on behalf of the will contest that her employer "sometimes repeated herself." The nurse was quick to admit that Bourne wasn't insane when she gave her money or the car, though.

The niece lost; Bourne's will would stand. Her fortune went to "institutions in the Town of Bourne, Mass.," the Bourne Workshop for the Blind in New York and a host of other deserving good works to help the infirm, widows, orphans and those in legal distress. She also gave money for a memorial to her brother, Jonathan Bourne Jr., in his adopted state of Oregon. She liked to have the family name attached to as many charities as possible, but she herself was quiet and unassuming; she'd attend each unveiling but would not actually speak.

Emily Bourne worked hard to use her family money for "the general benefit of humanity," so it's time she got some of the credit that she so lavishly bestowed on her father and brother.

3

NORTH FALMOUTH

NORTH FALMOUTH LIBRARY
6 CHESTER STREET, NORTH FALMOUTH, MA 02556
508-563-2922
WWW.FALMOUTHPUBLICLIBRARY.ORG

Public libraries are the sole community centers left in America. The degree to which a branch of the local library is connected to the larger culture is a reflection of the degree to which the community itself is connected to the larger culture.
—Russell Banks (b. 1940, American author)

There's a sunny, lighthearted feeling in North Falmouth Library. Maybe it's because the library staff understands how vital it is to engage with children early and get them excited to have contact with the library, either on trips to the library or having the staff visit them at their school or daycare center with story hours, activities and crafts. Just a few of the imaginative ways they attract kids include a Stuffed Animal Day Camp; a monthlong game of Candyland with game pieces hanging from the ceiling; and the Fun Friday Family Event, with a book club, board games and other family activities. The kids were entranced when their area of the library was transformed into a jungle to promote reading as an adventure.

It's a compact place, perhaps because the building was an abandoned barracks from the military base nearby; the books are well laid out, and it's good to get to know this pretty, out-of-the-way village, six miles north of Falmouth center. It has an interesting history.

The North Falmouth Public Library, a remodeled military barracks, is a village sweet spot. *Author's collection.*

Native Americans left their ancestral home here when European settlers moved in; there is a burial ground on a hill at the end of Cedar Lake off Old County Road that once had more than one hundred grave markers. This is right behind the library, in the Francis A. Nye Memorial Park, so it isn't possible to enlarge the library without further desecration of the grave sites. *Falmouth Enterprise* archives report that "the stones were unwittingly destroyed or removed in the early 1900s by workmen who were clearing brush from the area." While it may be true that Native American burial grounds did not usually contain typical tall, flat European-style headstones, neither does the word *unwittingly* have a loud ring of truth to it.

In 1924, the Town of Falmouth Parks Commissioners installed a marble marker declaring the area an Indian Cemetery. More recently, the Massachusetts Historical Commission confirmed the presence of artifacts there from 450 to 8,000 years ago.

As is true for much of Cape Cod, early arriving European families acquired enormous amounts of acreage and began their dynasties; the surnames of

Nye, Hatch and Hamblin are seen everywhere in North Falmouth on maps from 1635 to the present. Nine generations of Nye men were postmaster, justice of the peace, surveyors and politicians, along with fighting in the Revolutionary War. Nyes were ship captains out of local ports and New Bedford whaling ports, and others ran saltwater evaporation systems for curing meats and fish.

The first church was the North Falmouth Congregational Church, constructed in 1832. Fifteen Nye family members were among the founders, and all the church organists were Nyes for the entire first century of the church's existence. Lizzie Wheeler Nye, for instance, was the organist for fifty-five years. The church was in front of the existing North Falmouth Cemetery, and of the nineteen members who founded the cemetery, fourteen had the surname Nye.

For many years, the North Falmouth Library was in the basement and the balcony of the North Falmouth Congregational Church.

Weekly music and debates took place in Megansett Hall, 137 Old Main Road, from 1886 until 1926, when the building was purchased by a farming organization to use as the Megansett Grange. Entertainment continued there, however, with plays, dances, festivals and auctions. As the Cape Cod Railroad came through the village in 1872, the summer community aspect of North Falmouth accelerated, and with that came more entertainment, restaurants and general services for tourists. Henry Fonda and Jimmy Stewart performed in the University Players Guild summer theater at Silver Beach from 1929 to 1932.

Across from today's North Falmouth Library was the Megansett Tea Room at 13 Chester Street; it's now a private home. The North Falmouth Fire Station, built in 1915 at 212 Old Main Road, moved to the corner of Old Main Road and Wild Harbor Road in 1951. The North Falmouth Library took over the old fire station in 1956, but it is now the home of the North Falmouth Village Association, a civic group that organizes town events. The library has been on Chester Street since 1966.

Another transformation in the area was the Spencer Barn at 294 Old Main Road. Built in 1904 for William C. Spenser's prized Morgan horses, it was turned into a rowdy nightclub called the Banjo Room in the 1960s, causing regular ruckus in this quiet village. The Federal Housing Assistance Corporation bought it in 1989 and converted it into a homeless shelter for young women and first-time mothers in need of services.

Now listed on the National Register of Historic Places, the North Falmouth Village Historic District encompasses the civic buildings and grand old houses that still grace the winding streets along the ocean as well as the regular thoroughfares like Route 28A. Architectural preservation is important to most of the residents of North Falmouth.

A recent survey of patrons questioning their feelings about the North Falmouth Library, which is small and worthwhile, was also resoundingly positive. Everyone, it seems, wants North Falmouth Library to stay.

4

WEST FALMOUTH

WEST FALMOUTH LIBRARY
575 ROUTE 28A, WEST FALMOUTH, MA 02574
508-548-4709
WWW.WESTFALMOUTHLIBRARY.ORG

*The health of our civilization, the depth of our awareness about the
underpinnings of our culture and our concern for the future can all be tested by
how well we support our libraries.*
—Carl Sagan (1934–1996, astronomer)

With a sea of shining wood floors and islands of oriental rugs, West Falmouth Library is a gracious place. Started in the 1870s by five young women who longed for culture in this quiet farming community, it grew from a closet of fifteen books, purchased by collecting membership fees plus a nickel for every book checked out, to a collection of thirteen thousand housed in a beautiful building right across the road from the Quaker Meetinghouse.

The Young People's Union met weekly for music and literary events, at first in the home of Mary F. Gifford, then the Methodist Society vestry, and on to the second floor of the tag factory (which also has an interesting history; 400 locals tied pink strings onto merchandise tags in the late 1800s, earning 12 to 17 cents for each bundle of 1,010 successfully strung tags). When the tag factory burned down, villagers built a library on what is now Old Dock

The West Falmouth Public Library is the heart of the village. *Author's collection.*

Road; that building was picked up and moved to a site near the current West Falmouth Market, just a quarter mile away from its present location.

The West Falmouth Library Association replaced the Union in 1891, receiving its state charter in 1893. R.J. Mendenhall, a bank president and floriculturist from Minneapolis, along with his wife, Abby (Swift) Mendenhall, a West Falmouth village native, donated the land on which the library now stands. Local inventor D. Wheeler Swift, whose clever creations included envelope-making machines and laundry wringers, provided funds for the $5,000 building, which was completed in 1896. His 1910 will bequeathed a sum that provided financial stability for the library. An endowment fund was established in 1959 to further support it.

Because the mission of the West Falmouth Library is "To maintain a historic library building for the community, which is welcoming and accessible to all," accessibility of information is important here. Materials are available in various technological formats and for all ages. Thinking ahead, in 1997, the association bought a parcel next door to the library, calling it "Land for the Future." There's a beautifully designed and carefully tended place called Jane's Garden there now; visitors can ask at the circulation desk for a diagram identifying all the many perennials and herbs planted therein.

Like most Cape Cod villages, there's a great feeling of loyalty and historical fascination in West Falmouth, so the library considers it its job "to protect the cultural heritage of West Falmouth by collecting documents and items that reflect the people and events that have shaped the village." To that end,

> *The West Falmouth Library Archives collects and preserves archival materials pertaining to the history of the village of West Falmouth and the West Falmouth Library, including documents, photographs, correspondence, scrapbooks, newspaper clippings, oral history interviews, and realia* [three-dimensional objects from real life that do not fit into the traditional categories of library material, such as coins, tools and textiles]....*As the steward of primary and secondary sources, the Archives protects the heritage of the community, ensuring that it is available to the general public and future generations.*

Patrons can see the logbook of a whaling ship captain, Caleb O. Hamblin (1835–1907); oil paintings of long-ago community leaders; and the Bowerman-Gifford collection of papers from these two Quaker families, starting in 1673, along with additional ephemera.

The library is a nonprofit organization and does fundraising for about a third of its yearly budget. They have hosted a Murder Mystery Night with cocktails and hors d'oeuvres; a springtime Moveable Feast, featuring dinner at local homes and results of a silent auction held later that night at the library; a June village book sale; an art show and sale each July; and a House Tour and Boutique in the autumn.

West Falmouth has some small statistics—a population of under two thousand, its highest point is seven feet above sea level and it's only about four square miles—but it has several gorgeous beaches, stately vintage homes and a library that nurtures a sense of continuity and community.

5

WOODS HOLE

Woods Hole Public Library
581 Woods Hole Road, Woods Hole, MA 02543
508-548-8961
www.WoodsHolePublicLibrary.org

"You want weapons? We're in a library. Books are the best weapon in the world.
This room's the greatest arsenal we could have. Arm yourself!"
—Russell T. Davies (b. 1963, Welsh screenwriter and television producer)
in the science fiction series Doctor Who

Directly across the street from the Steamship Authority, where hooting, scenic ferries travel back and forth across Vineyard Sound between Woods Hole and Martha's Vineyard, is a lovely fieldstone building housing Woods Hole Public Library. Its companion, the Woods Hole Historical Museum, is next door. Public transportation from Falmouth is a good idea, especially during the summer months, as the entire village of Woods Hole has extremely limited (read: 140) metered parking spots. That dire warning duly expressed, it's worth the trip.

The Cape was one of the premier fishing areas of the Wampanoag people for thousands of years; the arrival of Bartholomew Gosnold in 1602 changed everything. He promptly gave Cape Cod the name that stuck for the ensuing four-hundred-plus years (because of all the cod here) and called Martha's Vineyard after his late daughter. He may have tried to stay in the good graces of the Native people, but it didn't last long; instead of the civil

Public Library, Woods Hole, Cape Cod, Mass.

A soldier wrote to his mother in 1944 on this postcard of Woods Hole Library. *The Walter "Red" Winn Collection/Nevins Memorial Library, Methuen, Massachusetts.*

trading of goods that the Wampanoag had come to expect from Europeans in their previous few encounters, Gosnold's men were hurriedly yanking up sassafras root and chopping down cedar trees to bring back to England, as these were known sources of profit. It didn't end well, and Gosnold sailed away within two weeks of setting foot on the mainland. Before he left, he declared the place Falmouth in honor of his hometown in England. It had been named Sucanessett by its original inhabitants, but it would be incorporated as Falmouth in 1686.

By then, European settlers had taken plots of sixty acres each in Woods Hole to raise sheep and crops. Next came the whalers and with them a village support system of candle makers, companies to process whale products and other shops to sell everyone food and clothing. When the whaling industry had destroyed itself by reckless overdoing, ships sailed for tiny islands off Peru to harvest guano (bird droppings) for use as fertilizer in U.S. fields. It was a dangerous and complex process; its effect on the environment and human health was deliberately ignored; and in less than thirty-five years the islands were destroyed, the bird population disappeared and plenty of poor workers suffered and died.

Two decent things came out of the debacle: the first was the establishment of the U.S. Commission of Fish and Fisheries, which came to Woods Hole in 1871 to study water health for our fish supply. The Marine Biological Laboratory was founded here in 1889, followed by the Woods Hole Oceanographic Institution in 1930.

The second benefit was train service, which was extended to Woods Hole in order to transport heavy loads of guano up to Boston and beyond. Trains also brought visitors, visitors brought money and some of that money was contributed by happy summer visitors to build the library. (The trains are long gone now, but at least the track bed was paved to become the Shining Sea Bikeway in 1974.)

Woods Hole Public Library began in 1873 as Woods Hole Social Library in the basement of Asa Shiverick's house. He was superintendent of the guano factory; the chief chemist, Azariah Crowell, was in attendance, as well as Josephine Swift, a member of the merchant and maritime family. They decided to issue eighty-nine shares at two dollars each and began buying books to supplement those they'd donated themselves.

Five years later, the Social Library moved to the basement of the brand-new Community Hall (which was called Liberty Hall) and stayed there until its book collection grew too large. In 1896, the library moved across the street to a building that was originally a Swift family house; however, the rent was too high at one hundred per year, so after two years, when the library was offered free space inside the Eliel T. Fish grocery store building, it was grateful to accept. It couldn't last forever, and it didn't—the store was sold in 1910, so the library was on the move again, but this time, after settling all its books in empty rooms in Woods Hole School, the whole village knew they needed to make a plan for a permanent library home.

The Massachusetts Library Commissioners Report from 1910 describes the good news well:

This library, which started in 1873 in the home of Asa Shiverick, is to have a handsome and convenient building, of granite boulders, on an elevated and conspicuous site, commanding a wide view of the ocean and the country. Several months ago friends of the library began planning for a building and started subscriptions. Many summer visitors were enlisted, more than $5,000 pledged, and a site secured. A building committee composed of H.K. Dyer, A.C. Harrison, and W.O. Luscombe obtained plans, which were accepted; and it is hoped to have the building ready for occupancy in the spring or early summer. The building is to be rectangular, with a deep L at the rear for a commodious stack room. The main part is a large reading room and directors' room, while from the front projects *a considerable vestibule. The inside finish will be weathered oak. Bound volumes, about 3,000; circulation, 2,652.*

The next three years were spent raising money, buying the land at 581 Woods Hole Road, drawing up building plans and incorporating as Woods Hole Public Library. All the books were systematically catalogued by the Massachusetts Free Public Library Commission and, finally, arranged in the new building in time for its opening in January 1913.

Two expansions have occurred since, in 1952 and 1990, doubling its size. The Woods Hole Historical Collection was founded in 1976 in Bradley House, next to the library. Twenty years later, two more buildings were incorporated into the library site: the Yale Workshop and the Swift Barn, which houses the Small Boat Museum. Now the whole amazing campus is called the Woods Hole Historical Museum. It features all kinds of interesting things like Wampanoag artifacts from the first people to live here; in fact, the museum makes this clear in its Land Recognition Statement:

> *The Woods Hole Historical Museum is located on the traditional and sacred land of the Wampanoag people who still occupy this land, and whose history, language, traditional way of life, and culture continue to influence Cape Cod.*

There are exhibits of photographs displaying the changes from whaling port to scientific research hub, a scale model of Woods Hole as it appeared in 1895 and numerous oral histories and information about houses and general life in the village. In 1981, Woods Hole Public Library was bequeathed a sum by Thomas G. Ratcliffe that established a library endowment. In 1990, a project was completed to renovate the building, making it handicapped-accessible; creating a children's room; and finishing a small room that houses the Thomas G. Ratcliffe Theatre Collection.

Woods Hole Public Library welcomed 20,000 visits and ran 265 programs for its patrons (pre-pandemic) in 2019. Its "Library of Things" to borrow includes a sewing machine, metal detector, telescope, ukulele, acoustic guitar, games, puzzles and even cake pans in a variety of fun shapes. The whole compound is one delightful surprise after another.

6

FALMOUTH

Falmouth Public Library
300 Main Street, Falmouth, MA 02540
508-457-2555
www.FalmouthPublicLibrary.org

*A library is a place that is a repository of information and gives every citizen
equal access to it. That includes health information.
And mental health information. It's a community space.
It's a place of safety, a haven from the world.*
—*Neil Gaiman (b. 1960, British author)*

All researchers owe a debt of gratitude to Falmouth Public Library
for its tireless pursuit of safeguarding historic documents. It is not
the only library to do this, but its collection is vast, the process
to secure funding arduous and the final result successful beyond measure
because it's accessible online.

The collection of incredibly important and irreplaceable items includes
handwritten captains' logbooks dating to 1806, town reports from 1884 on
and the *Falmouth Enterprise* from 1892; some were on microfilm already, but
many historic maps, registers (such as the Falmouth Survey of Old Houses
Historic Register) and directories that are necessary resources were at risk of
deteriorating. Students and teachers, future historians and genealogists need

Public Library and High School, FALMOUTH, Mass.

There's a box of historic goodies from 1901 under the cornerstone of Falmouth Public Library. *The Walter "Red" Winn Collection/Nevins Memorial Library, Methuen, Massachusetts.*

this information, whatever the cost. The thought of possibly losing Falmouth's past when it could have been saved was too dreadful to contemplate.

In the spring of 2005, Falmouth adopted the Community Preservation Act, Massachusetts General Law Chapter 44B, establishing a special fund of monies—the Community Preservation Fund—to be appropriated and spent for certain open space, historic resources and affordable housing purposes; in 2012, outdoor recreation was added to the list. Funds are raised locally by a voter-authorized surcharge on local property tax bills of up to 3 percent. Deed recording fees charged by the state's Registries of Deeds are the funding source for the statewide Community Preservation Trust Fund. Revenues from these two sources—the local CPA property tax surcharge and annual distributions from the state's Community Preservation Trust Fund—combine to form a town's Community Preservation Fund. After the town adopts the CPA, a local committee of five to nine members reviews applications for grants.

In 2006, the Falmouth Library Foundation funded a study to determine the process and cost of preserving the archive. A few years later, the foundation applied for, and received, a Community Preservation Fund grant. The foundation contributed more money to meet the actual cost of the project, and then the library started the time-consuming tasks of evaluating all the materials, repairing some of them and storing them in archival environments—acid-free and monitored for the correct temperature and humidity so further damage would be avoided. Then came planning how to best catalogue and digitize everything so anyone at home could find all these things on the library's website. By 2011, the foundation had completed this phase of the huge project, and an additional grant was applied for to implement the digitization (conversion of text, pictures or sound into a digital form that can be processed by a computer).

They were given the second grant from the Community Preservation Fund of about $204,000 and an additional $7,500 matching grant from the Horizon Foundation (horizonfoundation.org) to protect the library's treasured archives, which included Falmouth Annual Reports from 1865, 1872 and 1875 through 1882; Bourne, Falmouth and Sandwich directories from 1900 and 1903; 1880, 1910 and 1907 atlases of Barnstable County; the *Falmouth Enterprise* from 1896 to 1962; ships' logs; miscellaneous town records from 1668 to 1960; and miscellaneous library records from 1794 to the 1960s and beyond.

All of this work was published on the library's website in 2015 in a format that is easily searchable by the public. It is extremely interesting to browse editions of the *Falmouth Enterprise* from the past century, to see the flourish of beautiful handwriting in ancient ledgers, and to witness almost firsthand the evolution of Falmouth and the rest of Cape Cod—not just the news of the day but the culture and the spirit of community. The town has a long history in this regard.

The Falmouth Library Society began in 1792. Membership was one dollar per year, and the rules were plentiful, written in longhand on yellowed parchment; there were regulations about meetings, money and how books would be bought, catalogued and cared for. From "An Account of the Damages Done to the Library in 1795," there are the following crimes: "Stackhouse *History of the Bible Vol. 3*, two leaves torn by Samuel Palmer. Chart of Southern Hemisphere in Volume 1 of *Cook's Voige* [*sic*], torn by Silas Lawrence and afterwards torn quite off by Abial Eldred."

Subscription libraries full of dull scholarly works and almost exclusively male readers became less popular by the mid-1800s, so the next phase of libraries was called the circulating library. In theory, they were similar— books were borrowed for a fee, but at least the public was permitted to join without an invitation, and more importantly, women were not only allowed but also encouraged to take out books. Publishers saw a good opportunity to sell their wares at a discount to these libraries, whose patrons could be counted on to request sequels and additional titles in the same genres; both the library and the publisher would benefit. Fiction was the most sought-after reading material by far at this time, exactly what subscription libraries had little of to offer.

By 1876, the new Falmouth Circulating Library, founded by an enterprising group of women, provided a much broader spectrum of subjects and a larger collection in general. Its opening statement reads:

> *We, the undersigned, believing that a library judiciously selected is eminently useful for mental and moral culture, and that it offers ample means for said improvement and refinement, agree to establish our library association and adopt the following constitution and bylaws.*

The regulations still sounded a bit officious. From the Library Rules in 1877: "A fine of 25 cents shall be imposed upon any member or non-member who may loan a book, belonging to or taken from this library, to be carried to the residence of another person."

After the passage of the Massachusetts Library Act in 1891 and the establishment of a public library in Falmouth, the Circulating Library's two thousand volumes merged with the ninety-eight new books given by the state to form the Falmouth Free Public Library in Town Hall. Space was tight. The library fund had $3,000, bequeathed by Esther (Mrs. James M.) Beebe, so a new building at 300 Main Street was built—but not without some drama. From the *Enterprise*, October 6, 1900:

> *We are inclined to believe that the town made a great mistake at the special town meeting last Saturday afternoon in allowing the motion to be carried instructing the building committee not to exceed the original appropriation of $25,000. In order to build a two-story structure as per plans approved, $32,500 would be required, but if they were only allowed $25,000, a one-story building would have to be erected....We now have one of the finest locations in the village, and to erect a low, one-story building on that lot will be a disgrace to the future generations of our town....Falmouth has already become famous for its beauty and attractiveness; let us not cast a blot upon her....We want a building that will be an ornament to our town, now and for years to come. Citizens, think this over before it is too late.*

The new Falmouth Memorial Library was indeed built as it had been intended, two stories tall and nicely ornamental (in a classic, not flashy, way) as well as practical. It is a memorial to those who died in the Civil War. Construction ended up being even more expensive and took longer than expected. The laying of the cornerstone generated this sad blurb in the *Enterprise* from January 12, 1901:

> *The cornerstone of the Falmouth Memorial Library building was laid last Thursday morning. There was no ceremony attending the laying of it. The copper box which was placed under the stone was made and presented by Messrs. Lawrence & Hall of this village and contained the following articles:—Two special numbers of the* Enterprise, *two current numbers of the Boston daily papers, one copy of the* New Bedford Evening Standard *of December 3, 1900, containing President McKinley's*

The glass dome in Falmouth Public Library features the official seal of the Town of Falmouth. *Author's collection.*

message to congress, copy of the High School Pioneer, one copy Ancient History of Falmouth *by Jenkins, one copy* Celebration of Falmouth Bi-Centennial, *silver coins of 1900, picture of public library.*

By 1905, the library's collection had grown to 6,733 volumes. That year, Falmouth was chosen to host the annual meeting of the Massachusetts Library Club (the predecessor of the Massachusetts Library Association), which was founded in 1890 at the State Library in Boston. Meetings were held at a different location each time, and librarians enjoyed traveling around the state to these conventions.

Invitations were sent out well enough in advance to make plans. For instance, "The Meeting of the Massachusetts Library Club at Falmouth, Massachusetts, June 15–16, 1905," contained the following information:

> *The headquarters of the Club will be at Terrace Gables Hotel at Falmouth Heights.... The rate will be $2.00 a day. Arrangement has been made with T.L. Swift to take passengers to and from Terrace Gables at a fare of 10 cents each way. On Friday morning the party will drive to Woods Hole to visit the Marine Biological Laboratory and the Station of the U.S. Fish Commission. (Fare 50 cents.) Dinner may be had at the Avery House for 50 cents. The railroad fare from Boston to Falmouth, and return from Woods Hole, will be about $2.40. Tickets should be bought of the Secretary on the train.*

A local version of the state library club, the Cape Cod Library Club, was started in 1900 and continued through the 1970s. From the *Enterprise* of September 7, 1918:

> *Librarians, library trustees, and others interested in library work are urged to attend the meeting of the Cape Cod Library Club which is to be held at the Falmouth Free Public Library…when puzzling problems will be discussed. It is hoped that many people will take advantage of the opportunity to hear Mr. John Adams Lowe, president of the Massachusetts Library Club, who has had unusual experiences in connection with Library War Service, and Miss Edith Guerrier of Washington, D.C., who is a forceful and entertaining speaker.*

In the twenty-first century, the library has engaged in serious communication with its patrons to develop strategies consistent with its vision statement: "The Falmouth Public Library—where inspiration, imagination, innovation, and discovery come together enriching lives and creating a vibrant and informed community," and its mission statement, "The Falmouth Public Library engages and empowers the community through its programs, services, and its collections that inform, educate, and entertain."

Moving forward, this process will include community collaborations and connections; providing a place for discovery; offering excellence in service; and sustaining core responsibilities, which are to provide the community with free access to all collections and programs by removing all barriers, to be a trusted information source and community resource and to abide by state laws regarding patron confidentiality, the American Library Association Code of Ethics and Freedom to Read and Freedom to View.

7

EAST FALMOUTH

EAST FALMOUTH LIBRARY
310 ROUTE 28, EAST FALMOUTH, MA 02536
508-548-6340
WWW.FALMOUTHPUBLICLIBRARY.ORG

The library card is a passport to wonders and miracles, glimpses into other lives, religions, experiences, the hopes and dreams and strivings of ALL human beings, and it is this passport that opens our eyes and hearts to the world beyond our front doors, that is one of our best hopes against tyranny, xenophobia, hopelessness, despair, anarchy, and ignorance.
—Libba Bray (b. 1964, American author)

A homey library with a sunken, fireplaced living room is a wonderful place to read and admire the works by local artists dotting the walls and windows overlooking tranquil Mill Pond. In this location since 1971, the East Falmouth Library started in 1936 in a section of the East Falmouth School. From the front page of the *Falmouth Enterprise* on January 23, 1936:

> *The East Falmouth branch library, authorized by the 1935 town meeting, opened Tuesday afternoon in the East Falmouth School. More than 100 persons, mostly children with a sprinkling of adults, visited the spacious room, newly equipped with shelves and reading tables and stocked with*

The reading area of the East Falmouth Library offers a serene view of Mill Pond. *Author's collection.*

about 1,000 books from the main library, on opening day. Although a wide selection of books from the main library stacks, both fiction and non-fiction, have been placed in the new branch, [the librarian,] through the Enterprise, *issues an appeal for donations of books of all kinds. Good fiction, new or old, is most needed, but any worthwhile books will be appreciated. Book circulation at the branch on opening day was 100 out of a total of 1,000. The room housing the branch library is located at the northwest corner of the East Falmouth School, with an independent entrance on Davisville Road. The inner walls were fitted with shelves fashioned on the spot. Tables for reading, a magazine rack, a card file, and a librarian's desk have been provided.*

The East Falmouth Library was a success, circulating close to five thousand books in its first year; the librarian's yearly salary was $156. Just seven years later, it was closed "until further notice" during World War II, a combination of the school needing the space for kindergarteners along with transportation and heating problems due to fuel rationing.

When the new East Falmouth Elementary School was built, the branch library once again opened in the school and stayed there from 1963 to 1971—until both the school and the library needed more space. A private home was for sale on Mill Pond, and its owner had built it with an eye toward making it adaptable for commercial use; the interior walls, for instance, could be easily removed because they had no pesky wiring to get in the way. The town bought the property and converted it to a proper, permanent place for the East Falmouth Library.

In the past few years, eight stone benches—blocks from a granite flume that was part of a cranberry bog dam near John Parker Road in Falmouth—have been installed outside the library. There are marks on the blocks from a star drill hand tool that masons used over one hundred years ago. The granite benches and some wooden seating near the front door comprise a lovely reading garden for the East Falmouth Library's permanent home.

8

MASHPEE

Mashpee Public Library
64 Steeple Street, Mashpee, MA 02649
508-539-1435
www.MashpeePublicLibrary.org

The contents of a library can take you further than your own imagination could begin to imagine. To open a book is to open your mind.
—Amberle Cianne (b. 1994, American author)

Mashpee couldn't wait to take advantage of the Massachusetts Public Library Act of 1891; residents were certain it would pass, and they wanted to be well prepared when it did. Mary F. Holmes donated land in 1887 for the Mashpee Public Hall Library Society to build on, stipulating that the library must be built within one year of the passage of the Library Act. It was.

In fact, Mashpee was one of the first thirty-six towns to establish its library that year. The town received its $100 from the state to purchase books, then appropriated an additional $15; trustees were appointed, and finally the new library opened in 1892 in part of the Public Hall.

By 1928, the collection and residents' interest in it had grown so that the library needed its own dedicated building. Town Meeting set aside $1,625 for the project, and construction began at the corner of Snake Pond Road and Great Neck Road; Mashpee Public Library would spend the next forty years

Mashpee Public Library is twenty-two thousand square feet of sustainability and environmentally friendly design. *Author's collection.*

at that location. In 1967, a new library building was constructed on Great Neck Road, but by 1987, it had outgrown it—again. The fourth Mashpee Public Library, built on Steeple Street on the edge of Mashpee Commons, was nice, but the burgeoning population made it too small very quickly. In 2010, the town opened a beautiful new one.

The fifth rendition of Mashpee Public Library is a twenty-two-thousand-square-foot, state-of-the-art environmentally friendly building in Mashpee Commons (which has itself grown so much that the library is no longer on its edge). A pretty, swirling staircase leads up to the stacks, meeting rooms, study spaces and comfortable reading areas. This new library is as different from the previous one as it can possibly be, even though it's built on the same spot.

Books by and about the Wampanoag and other Native Americans are included in the Mashpee Public Library collection. *Author's collection.*

It's wonderful to see a large area dedicated to Native American materials. Considering how Cape Cod came to be renamed and owned by Europeans, most of whom, to this day, still refer to *themselves* on town history websites as the settlers and firstcomers here, it's refreshing that Mashpee remembers its *actual* roots and honors them.

Of course, the library isn't just books. Just a few of the Library of Things to borrow are mobile hotspots; a high-powered binocular microscope; a twelve-inch human body model with six removable organs; a birdwatching kit with binoculars; a metal detector; a Celestron Travel Scope; and twelve robot blocks to build robots.

Databases to use while visiting the library include Ancestry.com and ABCMouse. There are movies to watch using Kanopy, and magazines and newspapers such as *Consumer Reports* and the *Boston Globe*, the *Cape Cod Times*, the *Wall Street Journal* and the *New York Times*.

In partnership with AARP, free income tax preparation and filing services are available to patrons of any age. The library co-sponsors a series of successful programs with the Mashpee Historic Commission and secured funding to digitize the *Mashpee Enterprise* and preserve the town's history.

The Friends of the Mashpee Library create summer programs and fundraisers like author lectures, miniature golf tournaments and concerts, making money to buy sewing machines for weekly do-it-yourself and crafting events. Circulation here is very big—about 210,000 per year. The library offers 500 programs per year with a staggering 11,000 participants.

Mashpee Public Library seems to have taken to heart the Statement of Ambition adopted by the Public Library Association of America: "A dynamic public library is the heart of every community."

PART II

·

The Mid-Cape

9

COTUIT

COTUIT LIBRARY
871 MAIN STREET, COTUIT, MA 02635
508-428-8141
WWW.COTUITLIBRARY.ORG

The idea of a library full of books, the books full of knowledge,
fills me with fear and love and courage and endless wonder.
—Elizabeth McCracken (b. 1966, American author)

*P*uffy leather chairs face the fireplace, and a piano waits nearby for another tasteful musical program in Cotuit Library, tucked away in this scenic village south of Route 28. Over the mantel is a portrait of Sidney Kirkman, for whom this room is named. His generosity will figure into the library's story shortly.

The citizenry of 1800s Cotuit put forth valiant efforts to create this library. Using the Latin name for "a hall for public lectures, concerts and educational endeavors," popularized by Aristotle's method of teaching, the Cotuit Lyceum Society searched for a permanent home for its collection of books that had temporarily found shelf space in a Santuit store owned by Ronald Crocker, then the Asa Bearse store behind Freedom Hall, 976 Main Street, Cotuit.

The third attempt finally stuck: in 1895, the Cotuit Library Association bought the austerely named District 11 Schoolhouse from the village for

The Jane Reidy bench outside Cotuit Library features a Thoreau quote: "Live the life you've dreamed." *Author's collection.*

$800 and moved its books into what is now the entrance room. Architect Guy Lowell, who also designed the Boston Museum of Fine Arts, added iconic Ionic columns in the classical style to a new library front in 1901. After the Richard Gallagher addition in 1963 and the Sidney A. Kirkman extension in 1977, Cotuit Library is now a sprawling affair, carpeted and cozy and home to an inordinate number of community programs for its size.

Kirkman was a multimillionaire in the 1920s, having steered his grandfather's company, Kirkman & Sons (famous for Kirkman's Pure White Soap Flakes) from a smallish affair with eighty-five employees to almost four hundred workers in Brooklyn, New York. He sold the company to Colgate-Palmolive at a tidy profit in 1930. As an interesting side note, the unattractive

The Cotuit Library Association transformed an old school into a treasured community resource in 1895. *Author's collection.*

soap factory he bought in 1915 in a rather seedy section of Brooklyn was renovated ninety-nine years later into condominiums that sell for over $3 million each, and they come with the original rusty soap silos—colossal cylinders that reach from the basement up to the fifth floor. Naturally, they're now part of each residence's desirous design elements.

His generosity made possible the Sidney A. Kirkman and Mary Lewis Kirkman Fund in 1960, which has helped realize the Cotuit Library's goals (along with its own fundraising and some funds from the Town of Barnstable).

Several different book discussion groups meet here, along with game players and hobbyists; there are movies, concerts, handcrafts, author talks and other guest speakers and even educational luncheons provided by the Friends of Cotuit Library. The Cotuit Civic Association, the Historical Society of Cotuit and Santuit, the Cape Cod Writers' Club and the Precinct's Town Councilor gather at the library as well.

Community outreach is one of the library's hallmarks. The Barnstable Adult Community Center (formerly the Senior Center) has received free digital literacy and technology programs; these have been provided to local homeless shelters, too.

The Children's Room is particularly cheerful; tall windows and colorful displays brighten a (once in a while dreary) Cape Cod winter day. Children always enjoy summertime story times with a member of the Cape Baseball League's Cotuit Kettleers.

Its holdings of about fifty thousand materials include a special collection of vintage mysteries and classic science fiction, and there are a dozen internet-ready computers for the public to use, along with other office equipment like a printer, scanner, copier and fax machine. Cotuit Library recently competed for, and won, a grant to improve patrons' digital/technical literacy; "Libraries Transforming Communities: Focus on Small and Rural Libraries" is an initiative of the American Library Association in collaboration with the Association for Rural and Small Libraries.

Cotuit's year-round population of less than four thousand proves its library's motto true, making "Cotuit Library: The Heart of the Village."

10

MARSTONS MILLS

MARSTONS MILLS PUBLIC LIBRARY
2160 MAIN STREET, MARSTONS MILLS, MA 02648
508-428-5175
WWW.MMPL.ORG

Libraries always remind me that there are good things in this world.
—Lauren Ward (b. 1970, American singer and actress)

Medium-sized but mighty in creative programming, the Marstons Mills Public Library fairly hums with activity. It would have to, in order to keep up with its motto: "Meeting the informational, educational, recreational, and cultural needs of the community."

To that lofty end, an annual Teen Writers Conference draws best-selling authors of young adult literature from all over the country; the library co-sponsors the Marstons Mills Village House Tour with the local historical society; and volunteers from the library's Patchwork Educational Garden bring hundreds of fresh bouquets to residents "who could use a smile."

MMPL even joined forces with the National Seashore and Cape Wildlife Center for educational programs and the fostering of diamondback terrapin turtles. But the most dramatic and fascinating program must be its "Green library" initiative to showcase ecologically sound practices. Actual goats were brought to the library's designated land to munch away, clearing the space for a Pollinator Garden (which dovetailed nicely with its Library Beautification Plan).

Marstons Mills Library was built in 1893 and is now part of the Green Library Initiative. *Author's collection.*

But what about books? Aren't libraries supposed to be about reading books? Yes and no. Today's libraries are much more than reading materials. They function as an informational and transformational force in each community; thank goodness they've evolved in this way.

The village may seem peacefully quiet now, but its history tells a much louder story. First settled by Europeans in 1648, Marstons Mills immediately began its industrial life by producing quicklime, a substance necessary for mortar to harden, by gathering oyster shells from Prince Cove and firing them in lime kilns. There were fulling mills, too, which refined the wool from local sheep; a gristmill for grinding wheat, corn and barley; a sawmill that turned logs into boards; and even the manufacture of tar for waterproofing ship hulls, which were also made here.

The Marstons Mills Post Office housed the first seven shelves of books when fifteen villagers met to form the Marstons Mills Library Association during the summer of 1891. They met in Liberty Hall, 2150 Main Street, Marstons Mills, a Greek Revival building with a diamond-shaped window set in its angled entrance vestibule. In 1893, Robinson Weeks donated the piece of land next to Liberty Hall that became the home of the Marstons Mills Public Library.

Now the library has a circulation of close to sixty thousand per year, including books, magazines, audio CDs and mp3s; DVDs; e-book, audio and digital downloads; e-book readers; and databases, along with Wi-Fi internet access and specialized collections such as drama and theater arts, the Lilith Gordon Women's Poetry Collection, Susan Martin Speculative Fiction and a substantial selection of large print books.

There are lots of clubs meeting here, like book discussion groups in a plethora of genres, yoga classes, knitters and story times for the littles.

The Marstons Mills Public Library's slogan says it all: "You can borrow a book, but you get to keep the ideas."

11

OSTERVILLE

OSTERVILLE VILLAGE LIBRARY
43 WIANNO AVENUE, OSTERVILLE, MA 02655
508-428-5757
WWW.OSTERVILLEVILLAGELIBRARY.ORG

In principle and reality, libraries are life-enhancing palaces of wonder.
—Gail Honeyman (b. 1972, Scottish author)

Thank Thankful Ames for the Osterville Village Library; she started the process of its creation in 1873 by filling her dining room with books and inviting people in on Saturday afternoons to borrow them. This proved so popular that the library had to move to rooms in the elementary school, Dry Swamp Academy, off Main Street.

By 1879, a summer resident, William Lloyd Garrison Jr. (1838–1909), had begun campaigning for a dedicated library building that would be free for all. Garrison, the son of the abolitionist of the same name, was a devout social activist who opposed prejudice against African Americans and other minorities and supported women's rights and workers' rights. From his obituary in the September 20, 1909 *Hyannis Patriot*:

> Among the original trustees of our Public Library we find the first named is that of Mr. Garrison. At the dedication service held in the Methodist Episcopal church Dec. 30, 1881, his name is again mentioned first among

those making appropriate addresses. Indeed, it should be mentioned first, as he was its founder. From almost the first of his being here, a little more than thirty years ago, he saw the need of an institution of this character. He frequently visited the post office, which in those days was the favorite resort for men desiring to learn the news, but he did not consider either the wise and the otherwise who congregated there as capable of imparting intellectual culture and lessons in morals as would a good library....He was especially solicitous of the young and wanted a place where school children could supplement their studies beyond the possibilities of the ordinary public school. He desired not only reference books but books which would interest and at the same time fill the mind with good and pure thoughts and develop true manhood and womanhood....He loved our little village by the sea-side. He could have made another place his summer home had it not been for the fact that he had visited Wianno.

The new four-room library and reading room was built at Mulberry Corners, 846 Main Street, and opened to the public in January 1882. It was of Queen Anne architectural style, with several gables, and had a collection of over 1,200 books. It was officially incorporated as the Osterville Free Library Corporation in March 1882 (and changed its name to Osterville Village Library in 2012).

Reverend Edward Bourne Hinckley was the new librarian. His granddaughter Katherine Hinckley was later the librarian for thirty-nine years, retiring in 1956 at the age of seventy-nine.

By the 1950s, the library building was feeling its age, more space for materials and community rooms was needed and plans were underway to expand. Just a three-minute walk away was a building that had been a five-and-ten-cents store, on the corner of Wianno Avenue and West Bay Road, that would do nicely after a little renovation. It was dedicated on July 27, 1958. Additions and upgrades in 1968, 1989 and 2011 have brought the library from 8,500 to 20,000 square feet of space.

The new building has room for an enormous panoply of programs. Classes for "tweens and teens" include Building a PC, Beginner Coders, Intro to C+++ Programming, Science & Engineering and more. Other collaborations include Cape Community Media Center and EforAll. The Innovation Center features two Oculus Rift VR headsets, a Dremel 3D printer, a Green Screen, twelve high-end Dell gaming laptops and "Virtual Reality 'trips' for those who are otherwise unable to visit places such as the Ann Frank House, or climb Mount Everest, or have a front

The Osterville Village Library renovation expanded the building from 8,500 to 20,000 square feet in 2012. *Author's collection.*

row seat to the Apollo 11 moon mission." There's even a Digital Art and Design lab.

Traditional story hours are now STEM (science, technology, engineering, mathematics) Storytimes, where preschoolers engage in stories, crafts and hands-on STEM activities. In its expanded Makerspace area, children ages seven and older can experiment, problem-solve and create with STEAM (that's STEM plus the arts) materials. They can use and/or borrow robotic, coding and building kits and try out quality apps on the Makerspace iPad. More kits are available to learn about magnets, gears, time, snap circuit electronics, architectural drafting, origami, calligraphy, birdwatching with binoculars, sign language, bugs and other subjects. There are plenty of games and puzzles as well.

Starburst lights are a pretty feature of Osterville Village Library; its original 1882 sign hangs nearby. *Author's collection.*

Technology assistance with tablets, phones, e-readers and Mac and PC computers is available on a walk-in basis, seven days a week. Group training is also available.

The library arranges for free preparation and electronic filing of federal and Massachusetts income tax forms through AARP Tax-aide. In conjunction with the IRS, certified volunteers help low- and middle-income taxpayers. Osterville has a large collection of financial newspapers and periodicals (current): *Banker & Tradesman*, *Barron's*, *Investor's Business Daily*, *Wall Street Journal*, *Entrepreneur*, *Forbes*, *Harvard Business Review*, *Money* and *Value Line Investment*.

The staff plans numerous innovative events that become family traditions. The winter Christmas Stroll brings hundreds of people to the library to enjoy the lights on the lawn and have hot chocolate. Halloween celebrations involve lots of costumes, candy and an outdoor story walk. During a recent February vacation, kids enjoyed building a six-thousand-piece Lego replica of the Harry Potter castle. Free books are even provided year-round at Dowses Beach, 348 East Bay Road, in its Little Lending Library (a weatherproof cabinet filled with a variety of books to enjoy).

Their Library of Things includes a sewing machine, ukulele, kits for birdwatching and home energy saving, a garden soil meter, a digital photo converter, a Casio keyboard, a projector screen and even a meditation kit. There are Great Courses on national parks, computer programming, the night sky and birding. Patrons can access Ancestry.com, Mango Languages and a small business database.

The library's fundraising features several long-running annual events, such as the summer clam bake, a spring golf tournament, a car raffle and a road race. A more recent one is the annual Mutts and Martinis "Yappy Hour," with dog-friendly entertainment like a dog masseur, a pet artist, agility training and a dog acupuncturist. The humans manage to enjoy the time, too.

12

CENTERVILLE

CENTERVILLE PUBLIC LIBRARY
585 MAIN STREET, CENTERVILLE, MA 02632
508-790-6220
WWW.CENTERVILLELIBRARY.ORG

A library in the middle of a community is a cross between an emergency exit, a life-raft, and a festival. They are cathedrals of the mind; hospitals of the soul; theme parks of the imagination. On a cold rainy island, they are the only sheltered public spaces where you are not a consumer, but a citizen instead.
—Caitlin Moran (b. 1975, British journalist)

In 1846, a liberal thinker named Sylvanus Jagger had the audacity to discuss his ideas inside the Congregational Church in Centerville; this being frowned on, he took it upon himself to convince other freethinkers in the village to build a place where it would be safe "for every man" to express his thoughts on any subject. Liberty Hall was constructed forthwith and fulfilled its purpose for the next thirty years. When the number of open minds couldn't fit inside anymore, the building was sold and moved to a nearby farm to store cranberries; a new hall went up in 1877. The mastermind of the plan and of raising funds for it, Ferdinand Kelley, called the new place Howard Hall after his son-in-law, Howard Marston. Meanwhile, a village meeting in 1869 had framed a constitution to build a public library.

Schoolteacher Eugene Tappan started the endeavor in Moses Hallett's general store, where it stayed until 1877, when the handful of books were moved to the wheelwright shop of Nelson Phinney; it paused there for only a year before moving to the anteroom of the aforementioned Howard Hall while the books waited for their permanent (so Centerville thought) home to be built. From 1881 to 1897, they stayed in that edifice, which became too small because the Centervillians (402 in 1883) were too enamored of reading, so the collection kept growing.

In *Old Home Week Celebration, August 19–22, 1904: Historical Notes*, it was declared that a whole new library building was erected next door to Howard Hall with "both old and young contributing money and labor," opening for business in August 1897 at 565 Main Street. It was of a most endearing wooden architectural style, complete with a sloping eyebrow window peeking out of the roof. After more than fifty years, the pretty library was picked up and moved around the corner onto Church Hill Road to live out the rest of its life as a parsonage.

A new Centerville Public Library at 585 Main Street joined the long list of locations, and here it has stayed since 1956, when Charles Lincoln Ayling, in memory of his father, gifted the construction of the brick-arched building. Additional spaces along the decades include the Walter Lippmann Reference Room, the Phyllis Jerauld Bearse Children's Room, the Orr Room in honor of Dorothy Winship Orr and the Benjamin & Clara Edwards Children's Room. The library became ADA (Americans with Disabilities Act) compliant in 2014 with another 4,700 square feet of floor space, an elevator, ramps and other improvements.

Only a kind, appreciative staff can manage to keep a group of more than one hundred volunteers happy to help with library operations, so Centerville Library benefits from both.

Circulation in Centerville is well over 173,000, with a collection topping 35,000. More than 4,000 people come to 600 programs, and that's just for the adults. The library hosts podcasts; games like bridge, mahjong and chess; art classes; a writers' group; yoga; book discussion groups; knitting circles; and health talks. Some 500 more activities bring in another 6,000 children and teenagers each year. There's even a monthly Coffee House with singers, musicians and poets. Private technical assistance is extremely popular—from a volunteer computer expert who supplied more than 1,000 hours in just one year recently.

Strong libraries welcome collaborations. One of many is its recent collab with an Eagle Scout, who planted a butterfly garden to improve

A portrait of a book-loving cat hangs above the fireplace in Centerville Library. *Author's collection.*

the ecosystem by enticing pollinators into the outdoor area of the library with nectar plants. He also installed a house for the insects—a safe place for the butterflies to rest while being protected from the elements. All very educational and fun to watch, and all of it supports the library's motto: Read, Learn, Inspire.

13

WEST BARNSTABLE

WHELDEN MEMORIAL LIBRARY
2401 MEETINGHOUSE WAY, WEST BARNSTABLE, MA 02668
508-362-2262
WWW.WHELDENLIBRARY.ORG

*I always knew from that moment, from the time I found myself at home in that
little segregated library in the South, all the way up until I walked up the steps
of the New York City library, I always felt, in any town, if I can get to a library,
I'll be OK. It really helped me as a child and that never left me.*
—*Maya Angelou (1928–2014, American author, poet and civil rights activist)*

Two red bookcases and a feisty schoolteacher were the catalyst one
hundred years ago that started the Whelden Memorial Library in
West Barnstable. The Barnstable Town Report of 1949 reminisced:

*When big boys of the 1850s, '60s, and '70s were turbulent under men
teachers, Miss Martha Lee Whelden was brought to schools in Barnstable
and Yarmouth to quickly set schools to rights and establish a high standard
of order in the school room.*

Knowing her penchant for instilling good reading habits in her charges,
a friend of Whelden, Mrs. George Linder of Newton, donated books to
her school; at first, the older grammar school girls were in charge of this

Whelden Memorial Library is named for a no-nonsense nineteenth-century schoolteacher. *Author's collection.*

tiny lending library on the red shelves. It grew into the Linder Library Association in 1899. Volunteers constructed a new library on the corner of Lombard Lane and Meetinghouse Way in 1905, where it still stands—with a heartwarming weathervane of a boy reading to his dog. After Whelden and her sisters bequeathed $8,000 to it in 1923, the building was enlarged and renamed the Whelden Memorial Library.

It's a fitting tribute. Indeed, by all accounts Martha Lee Whelden was a formidable figure in West Barnstable history. The Cape Cod Library Club historian Caroline R. Siebens recalled fondly in 1952,

> *I remember very distinctly Miss Martha Whelden, who had charge of the girls from the State Industrial School* [the first reform school for girls in the country], *who served as maids in many Cape families. Miss Whelden*

made periodic visits to inspect their progress. She drove down in a buggy drawn by her fat little horse. With her bonnet tied over her carefully curled side locks, with her shawl of Paisely [sic] make, she was very impressive—not only to the maids, but to the small daughter of the household.

West Barnstable was the birthplace of another outspoken woman— Mercy Otis Warren, who wrote satirical essays and dramatic plays criticizing British policies in the years leading up to the Revolutionary War. She supported the boycotting of British goods and the Boston Tea Party and wrote *History of the Rise, Progress, and Termination of the American Revolution* in 1805. It was one of the first nonfiction works published in the United States that was written by a woman.

True to its motto of "Preserving and Promoting the Heritage of the Community," today Whelden Library houses twenty thousand materials and circulates double that, offers access to online genealogical database subscriptions, has indexed the sixteen volumes of West Barnstable history and holds numerous imaginative programs for children. It claims to have one of the largest circulating collections of materials on beekeeping, and another fun quirk is its collection of Finnish books. (In the late nineteenth and early twentieth centuries, many immigrants from Finland arrived here and settled in the eastern portion of the village.)

Outside there's a Little Black Pantry next to the patio benches—a set of black drawers for people to bring nonperishable food items to share with the community. The library's website explains, "Give or take. If you have less than you usually do, take. If you have more than you need, give. Thank you!"

¹4

BARNSTABLE VILLAGE

STURGIS LIBRARY

3090 MAIN STREET (ROUTE 6A), BARNSTABLE, MA 02630

508-362-6636

WWW.STURGISLIBRARY.ORG

I want to congratulate librarians, not famous for their physical strength or their powerful political connections or their great wealth, who, all over this country, have staunchly resisted anti-democratic bullies who have tried to remove certain books from their shelves, and have refused to reveal to thought police the names of persons who have checked out those titles. So the America I loved still exists, if not in the White House or the Supreme Court or the Senate or the House of Representatives or the media. The America I love still exists at the front desks of our public libraries.
—*Kurt Vonnegut (1922–2007, American author)*

It feels like a dignified old house because it is. The English founder of Barnstable, Reverend John Lothrop, had the house built in 1644, and as such, it's one of the oldest surviving homes on Cape Cod. More superlatives include being "the oldest structure still standing in America where religious services were regularly held." The quotation marks indicate the need for literalness, not interpretation, because there are numerous buildings in competition for the title and some others might try to fudge it, just a bit.

Not Sturgis Library, though. As the titleholder of "the house which forms the original part of the Library is the oldest *building* housing a public library in the United States," it is careful indeed to not step on the toes of those other libraries that claim to be America's oldest public library in continuous service since 1743; the first tax-supported free public library; the first publicly funded library in the United States; the first publicly supported free municipal library in the world; the oldest county library in the United States; or just plain America's first lending library. Beyond mild entertainment, there seems little point in contentious contests. Dignity and actual book-borrowing are more important, aren't they?

Sturgis Library, named for William Sturgis, who was born in this house in 1782 and a descendent of Reverend John Lothrop (1584–1653), is a splendid example of Colonial architecture, with beamed ceilings and wooden floors that are just a trifle slopey. There's a four-hundred-year-old Bible of Reverend Lothrop's in a microclimate display case, Currier & Ives lithographs of clipper ships and every sort of antique wooden furniture pieces throughout the library.

At fifteen, William Sturgis went to sea, ended up owning a fleet of clipper ships that sailed to and from China and bequeathed this house and $15,000 in bonds to create the library, which opened in 1867. Now, collections of Cape Cod history in several media, maritime history with a special emphasis on local sea captains (think ships' logs and diaries) and the Lothrop Genealogy Collection, comprising much sought-after information for researchers across the United States, are also housed in these handsome rooms. Sturgis Library is on the National Register of Historic Places.

But it's a modern library, of course, with the latest best-sellers and access to e-books and a fun Library of Things to borrow, like a telescope and a ukulele, as well as ongoing programs, book groups and art exhibits.

One unique feature of Sturgis Library is its Kurt Vonnegut Collection. Vonnegut lived in Barnstable Village, on the corner of Route 6A and Scudder Lane quite near the library, and served on its Board of Trustees in the 1960s. The twentieth-century novelist was best known for his books *Slaughterhouse-Five*, *Breakfast of Champions* and *Cat's Cradle*. The Sturgis Library Archives collection includes a first-edition copy of his work *Welcome to the Monkey House*, signed prints by his friend Morley Safer, a Kurt Vonnegut "Little Thinker" doll and numerous newspaper and magazine articles written by or about him.

The library is a fascinating museum, offering a self-guided tour with printed sheets to explain the myriad of historical objects and artwork

STURGIS LIBRARY, BARNSTABLE, MASS.

The Sturgis Library building dates to 1644. *Sturgis Library Archives*.

throughout the two floors. There are brilliant, moody oil paintings of Lothrops, Sturgises and many others; a slice of mulberry tree that stood outside the library for more than 150 years; antique maritime maps and artifacts; and even a red leather and carved oak nineteenth-century American Renaissance Revival chair that belonged to Samuel Hooper, William Sturgis's son-in-law, when he served in the U.S. House of Representatives.

One of the best things about this library is knowing that its original owner found peace here after being brutalized for years in a British jail. Reverend Lothrop came from a wealthy family, attended Oxford and Cambridge Universities and was ordained in the Church of England, where he preached for eleven years. When Lothrop became disenchanted with the doctrine and started his own church in 1623, the First Independent Church of London, King Charles the First had him arrested and thrown into the worst part of the worst prison: the Clink (yes, that's where the nickname for jail comes from). All he had to do was swear an oath of loyalty to the Church of England to avoid this, but he refused. After several years, Lothrop's wife died, leaving their seven children alone, so the king released the reverend on the condition that he get out of England and take his family and his followers with him.

He did. He sailed into Boston in 1634 with an entourage of thirty and set up a church in Scituate, but after five years of squabbling over doctrine, he

The Lothrop Room in Sturgis Library, Barnstable Village. *Author's collection.*

left the endless debating behind and went to Cape Cod, settling in Barnstable. Finally, he found the tranquility he'd been searching for in this beautiful village. With his new wife, whom he married in 1635, he had five more children. Most of John Lothrop's twelve children went on to have many children and so on; therefore, his direct descendants are vast in number and include, in addition to the non-famous ones, Ulysses S. Grant, Franklin D. Roosevelt, George Bush Sr. and Jr., Clint Eastwood, Oliver Wendell Holmes, Dr. Benjamin Spock, Mitt Romney, Adlai Stevenson, Mormon leader Joseph Smith, Henry Wadsworth Longfellow, Nathaniel Hawthorne, Eli Whitney and Georgia O'Keeffe.

William Sturgis had his own frightening adventures. As a trader between Alaska and China in 1809, his ship was attacked by pirates whose reputation for viciousness was all too warranted. Sturgis had four cannons with him in case pirates tried to board; he planned to blow up his own ship so his crew could not be tortured to death. Sturgis was able to hold the pirates off with cannon fire long enough to reach the safety of the harbor. He and his crew survived.

The following year, he went home to Boston; became involved in railroads, finance and politics; married; and eventually had six children. When he died in 1863, he bequeathed his family home to become the Barnstable Public Library—now called Sturgis Library.

15

HYANNIS

HYANNIS PUBLIC LIBRARY
401 MAIN STREET, HYANNIS, MA 02601
508-775-2280
WWW.HYANNISLIBRARY.ORG

If this nation is to be wise as well as strong, if we are to achieve our destiny, then we need more new ideas for more wise men reading more good books in more public libraries. These libraries should be open to all except the censor. We must know all the facts and hear all the alternatives and listen to all the criticisms. Let us welcome controversial books and controversial authors. For the Bill of Rights is the guardian of our security as well as our liberty.
—President John F. Kennedy

Rosella Ford Baxter, whose late husband, Sylvester, had been a sea captain, gathered fourteen women at her Main Street, Hyannis home in 1865 to discuss forming a subscription library in the village. Her friends were enthusiastic and immediately made plans to raise money, beyond the annual one-dollar dues, with which to buy books; eventually, funds were earned from selling cakes, doughnuts, tatting and other handcrafts. The book collection of the Hyannis Literary Association would be kept on shelves in Freeman Tobey's General Store on Pleasant Street.

PUBLIC LIBRARY, HYANNIS, MASS.

Hyannis Free Public Library on a postcard, circa 1910. *The Walter "Red" Winn Collection/ Nevins Memorial Library, Methuen, Massachusetts.*

These reminiscences about keeping books in a general store were recorded in the 1952 Cape Cod Library Club booklet:

> *The books were placed on shelves alongside packages of beans, coffee, and sugar, and grocery customers would loiter with their baskets on their arms to read a book or two in front of the store stove. Pretty soon the books began crowding out the beans and coffee and molasses jugs. So the library removed to the Saturday Night Club building, the one civic gathering place of the town, where checker clubs met and fiddle-dances were held.*

The collection stayed in the old Saturday Night Club, 257 Main Street, for a few years and then moved to its present location in 1908. The house it occupies had a long history too. Built around 1750, it belonged to Postmaster Otis Loring in the 1830s and doubled as the post office. In the 1840s, it was bought by Captain Samuel Hallett and his wife, Dorcas; when they died, their heirs sold the house to James Otis of Hyannis Port, who paid $2,500 for it and then gave it to the library as its permanent home.

Ora Adams Hinckley was the first full-time librarian in Hyannis and served from 1909 to 1943. She wrote in the *Barnstable Patriot* just before she died,

Shortly after the formation of the Hyannis Literary Association a benefit entertainment was held and $300 became available for the purchase of books. Oh! The excitement and joy of selecting them. Fancy the array of them! Bindings were not as attractive as those of today. Print and illustrations were not as alluring. There were meetings devoted to the work of getting them in readiness for circulation. They were, as was the custom then in public libraries, covered in brown paper. Thus jacketed they lost their outward individuality. They were all alike on the shelves. Covering the books was kept up until 1895, when by a vote of the association, the brown covers were removed.

Mrs. Hinckley was a direct descendent of John Alden and Priscilla Mullins and also President John Adams. Her husband, S. Alexander Hinckley, was a native Cape Codder and Civil War solider. In appreciation of her long service and popularity, the original Otis house, sometimes referred to as the Loring-Hallett-Otis House, was renamed in her honor. It's now the Ora A. Hinckley Building.

The Cape Cod Library Club, formed in 1900, held its annual meeting on September 21 and 22, 1933, in Hyannis; as it happened to be the library's twenty-fifth anniversary in the Loring-Hallett-Otis House, a large cake with twenty-five candles was part of the festivities. The yearly convention was always a happy occasion for participants:

After a two days' respite, Cape Cod librarians were back at their desks on Saturday afternoon and with smiling faces and new zeal for their tasks. They had been in attendance at Hyannis at the annual meeting of the Cape Cod Library Club, where they made contacts with one another, exchanged experiences, helped one another solve problems, and rejoice in each other's successes.…The place chosen was Lewis Bay Lodge.…There's not a prettier spot around.…In attendance it was a large meeting. Fifty sat at dinner on Thursday evening and others joined them for the program which followed. As many were present on Friday.

Thirty years after moving into 401 Main Street, the collection—and the population—had increased so much that an addition was built onto the right side of the library. Hyannis innkeeper Edward L. Eagleston donated $8,000 for the construction of the wing, and it was named for him.

In 1974, the library's trustees waged an extensive capital campaign to construct another building connected to the Eagleston Wing—this time a

Hyannis Public Library's modern addition lights up the night sky off of Main Street. *Author's collection.*

large, two-story, contemporary edifice. Quite different from the quaint Cape Cod houses that comprised the rest of the library, the Twombly Wing (funds bequeathed by Raymond and Florence Twombly) surprised some villagers with its design. However, from Main Street the library looks like it always did; the modern addition and entrance are behind the older buildings.

Hyannis Public Library provided 346 programs for children in 2019: story hours, Pokémon club, coloring and Lego groups, visits by members of the Companion Animal Program, meeting with Hyannis Harbor Hawks athletes and performances by the Bright Star Theatre Group. There were art sessions for those with special needs. Adults took part in book discussion groups and knitting groups, among others. In partnership with its next-door neighbor, the John F. Kennedy Hyannis Museum, the library presented a summer speaker series recently that was well-received.

In addition to books, magazines, audiobooks, DVDs and music, the library has many online databases. For instance, AtoZ Food America is for cooks, culinary students and historians. AtoZ the USA provides a resource for understanding the country's people, history, economy, geography, symbols, culture and society. AtoZ World Culture is an online database of information about the culture, language, history, food and religion for 175 countries. AtoZ World Travel contains 202 travel guides. The Black Freedom Database features select primary source documents related to critical people and events in African American history. The *Cape Cod Times* online database has current and past issues of Cape Cod's daily newspaper. Issues of *Consumer Reports* are available online, along with EBSCO Learning Express Library, Brainfuse's HelpNow and Brainfuse's JobNow database. Mango Languages for libraries offers over seventy world language courses. NewsBank is for news, NoveList Plus will help answer the question of what to read next and YALSA Teen Book Finder is a free online database and app to access nearly four thousand titles on a smartphone.

The library is particularly interested in ensuring that educational needs of children, young adults and their families are met, so the staff arranges library visits for teachers and students and outreach to public and private schools, daycare facilities and homeschooling groups.

16

WEST YARMOUTH

WEST YARMOUTH LIBRARY
391 MAIN STREET (ROUTE 28), WEST YARMOUTH, MA 02673
508-775-5206
WWW.YARMOUTHLIBRARIES.ORG

What in the world would we do without our libraries?
—Katharine Hepburn (1907–2003, American actress)

The year 1891 was a big one for Cape Cod libraries, as the State of Massachusetts had passed the Library Act, encouraging every town to build a library and giving them various incentives, such as one hundred dollars worth of books, to do so. West Yarmouth Library Association charter members met on January 12 to form the association "for the purpose of the establishment and maintenance of a library in West Yarmouth." They filled out forms and were formally incorporated on February 4, 1891, though the group had existed as a reading association since 1871.

The new, official library's books would be housed in half of the second floor of the village schoolhouse, on the same plot of land as it sits today. First through sixth grades had classrooms on the first floor, and seventh and eighth grades shared half the second floor; the rest of the second floor was for the West Yarmouth Library. The collection started with four hundred donated books, loaned to residents and "strangers" for $0.01 or $0.02 per

Though it began as a small reading association, West Yarmouth Library was fully incorporated in 1871. *Author's collection.*

week. (Later the term *strangers* was changed to "summer guests.") The library was open just one hour per week; dues were $0.50 per year, and the librarian was paid $10.00 per year.

The association met once each year to discuss circulation, fundraising and any other issues that might arise. The following cryptic announcement appeared in the January 4, 1896 *Yarmouth Register*: "The annual meeting of the West Yarmouth Library Association will be held this evening at 7 o'clock, at the usual place." By August, the *Register* was reminding people how generous the library hours were: "The West Yarmouth Library Association is open every Saturday from 3 o'clock until 4. The town's people and our visitors will bear in mind that there is good reading here for leisure moments."

By 1899, the loan fees had been abolished, which was seen to increase readership immediately. The town owned and maintained the building, but it was up to the association to buy books with funds realized from holding bazaars and bean suppers. The Town Dog License Tax helped; in 1906, the selectmen voted to appropriate $60 (one-third of the dog license tax) to the West Yarmouth Library. In 1928, the librarian's yearly salary rose to $50.

When the schoolchildren transferred to a different school in 1932, the library moved downstairs to the main floor, where, after extensive renovations, it stayed peacefully for the next thirty-three years. Anonymous donors, who later were revealed to be A. Harold and Frances Castonguay, offered funds to build and equip a new library on the same site (first moving the old school elsewhere) and then give the library to the town.

More than six hundred guests came to the West Yarmouth Library's Open House in April 1965. The new building gave the library new life; on July 22, 1968, 535 books were checked out during a single four-hour period. With this popularity and the many programs the library conducted, such as story hours, afternoon teas and educational endeavors, the village had a new center.

The West Yarmouth Library Association is now a group of Friends of the Library to raise funds for materials and programs not in the library's operating budget. With its support, the West Yarmouth Library provides craft programs, hosts summer reading programs and invests in technology and online resources. In addition, the association funds museum passes, library furniture and Volunteer Appreciation Day. With South Yarmouth Library Association, it hosts "The Who-ville Express," a December trolley ride between the two libraries that culminates in a reading of *How the Grinch Stole Christmas*. Regular fundraising projects include the Book Sale Shelf at the West Yarmouth Library and the outdoor book, hotdog lunch and craft sale in conjunction with the Cape Cod Village Crafters each summer.

17

YARMOUTH PORT

Yarmouth Port Library
297 Main Street (Route 6A), Yarmouth Port, MA 02675
508-362-3717
www.YarmouthPortLibrary.org

*You build a thousand castles, a thousand sanctuaries, you are nothing;
you build a library, you are everything!*
—*Mehmet Murat ildan (b. 1965, Turkish playwright)*

*I*s it significant that the self-proclaimed strangest inhabitant of Yarmouth Port, the late author and illustrator Edward Gorey, loved this library and it now holds a prized collection of his life's work?

…Probably. Gorey, responsible for the macabre but funny pen-and-ink drawings of the introduction to the PBS television show *Mystery!*, no doubt found images of the original incarnation of the building just perfect for his brand of humor—a fitting place for his quirky legacy to rest when he did, in 2000. The author of scores of hilariously illustrated books, such as *The Gashlycrumb Tinies* and *The Haunted Tea-Cosy*, lived at 8 Strawberry Lane, a quarter mile from Yarmouth Port Library. His house is a museum now; the library offers discount admission passes.

The Gothic/Second Empire architecture of the Yarmouth Port Library was completed in 1871 in a style quite unheard of today in library design; almost all new libraries are designed to be, or look, spacious and friendly. The

Public Library, Yarmouthport, Mass.

Pub. by R. H. Harris.

Yarmouth Port Library was a handsome example of Second Empire/American Gothic architecture in 1871. *The Walter "Red" Winn Collection/Nevins Memorial Library, Methuen, Massachusetts.*

Yarmouth Port Library's look was a little spooky, a little intimidating, high on a hill above Main Street (also called Route 6A). Even on its dedication it was somewhat controversial. Carol R. Siebens wrote in the 1952 Cape Cod Library Club pamphlet,

> *This same Gothic style, so prevalent in that time, was much condemned by a recent writer in the Library Journal as being bad architecturally and unfitted for library purposes! In my girlhood I considered this brick building with its towers and wrought iron staircases as the most elegant I had ever seen and quite looked down on the simple Cape Cod house of the Hyannis Library; why, I lived in just such a common ordinary house myself!*

Sadly, parts of the magnificent structure became unsafe by 1945 and had to be torn down; the rest was modernized in the 1950s, with wings named for John Simpkins and Mary Thacher, and more space was created in 1983 for a genealogy room and offices. It was, and is, a major social draw in Yarmouth Port. While in past decades elderly patrons gathered here for coffee and companionship weekly, now they have a number of educational, technological and hobby-related programs in addition to just meeting for a good chat.

There had been a subscription library in Yarmouth for ten years, 1807 to 1817. This Union Library charged yearly dues, and patrons bought shares; only brand-new books were purchased for the collection. Out of sixty-three members, three were women.

In 1866, another subscription library started in Yarmouth, this time by twenty men who met at the home of Charles Swift, the editor of *The Register* newspaper. Shares were ten dollars each; a small building (a former law office) was moved to a plot of land where the library now stands, given by Henry C. Thacher, and William J. Davis was the first librarian.

Yarmouth native Nathan Matthews didn't like the idea of a subscription library; $10 was way too much money for most people to spend on reading at that time. He offered to build a library worth $5,000 on the same property on the condition that it would be free for everyone in Yarmouth to use it. The twenty men agreed to relinquish all rights as shareholders. The little law office was turned into a kitchen for the librarian's apartment. Construction of the new Yarmouth Port Library was completed in 1871; the dedication took place on December 20 in the First Congregational Church, and then everyone took a tour of the building.

Yarmouth's villages are extraordinarily different. South Yarmouth and West Yarmouth have Route 28's lively commercial hustle and bustle while Yarmouth Port is quiet and historic. Driving east down Old King's Highway (Route 6A) in Yarmouth, look for a black oval plaque with a gold carving of a schooner on the houses that comprise the Captains' Mile. Each house with a schooner plaque was once owned by a real sea captain, some dating back to the 1600s, and all of them are carefully preserved. (They are private homes, so don't even think about stopping to look in the windows.) Only one is an actual museum: the Captain Bangs Hallet House at 11 Strawberry Lane in Yarmouth Port. The fifty-plus plaques have been awarded by the Historical Society of Old Yarmouth.

"Under the Spiral Staircase" is the location-descriptive name of the library's used book sale. Additional features of the library include three public computers with internet access; computer and device assistance; the Zinio app to download magazines; travel guidebooks and DVDs; language CDs; genealogy materials plus access to Ancestry.com (library edition); Cape Cod maps and guides to local attractions; book discussion groups; and special programs for children year-round.

As in several other Cape Cod towns, the issue of operating multiple village libraries instead of having one central facility also plagued Yarmouth for a time. The Yarmouth Port Library had remained privately funded since

The Yarmouth Port Library now, after renovation in the 1950s. *Author's collection.*

its inception, but in the 1990s the town began assisting each of the three libraries financially; the economic downturn in 2008 caused the Yarmouth Library Board to withdraw all town financial support and vote to close the Yarmouth Port Library.

Through the monumental efforts of the Yarmouth Port Library Association, negotiation with the town for a few extra months of time to work out the details and a full-scale fundraising drive, enough money was collected to keep the library open as a privately funded library, free to everyone.

18

SOUTH YARMOUTH

SOUTH YARMOUTH LIBRARY
312 OLD MAIN STREET, SOUTH YARMOUTH, MA 02664
508-760-4820
WWW.YARMOUTHLIBRARIES.ORG

When in doubt go to the library.
—J.K. Rowling (b. 1965, British novelist)

L ibrary floors should be a little creaky, if they've been properly trodden on for at least one hundred years—so this proves the popularity of the South Yarmouth Library.

The long road to having its own permanent home was bumpy and meandering, but finally, the *Yarmouth Register* could report some great news for library lovers on January 12, 1935:

> *On Monday, Jan. 7, the South Yarmouth Library association became owner of the Main Street property for which negotiations have been pending for several months, most of the delay in the proceedings being caused by the fact that one of the owners was a resident of Switzerland.*
>
> *The house which will in a few months, after needed repairs and alterations have been made, become the new home of the library, has long been intimately associated with the community life. It is a real Cape Cod dwelling though somewhat changed from its original outline. It is near most of the business activities of the village and its location will, doubtless,*

A pump and horse trough from 1885 is outside the South Yarmouth Library on Old Main Street. *Author's collection.*

enable it to serve a larger number of persons than it would reach within an equal radius in any other part of the village. This is especially true since the school library has taken on increased size and efficiency.

Let us glance at the history of this recently-acquired property. Barnstable records show that in 1816 Samuel Farris conveyed to Zeno Killey an acre of land which included these premises and extended from the "road to Farris' mill" to the land belonging to School District No. 7. Four years later, Zeno Killey deeded to Ebenezer Hallet, Jr. the same tract. The latter evidently did some building and conducted a tannery for, when he mortgaged to Thomas Akin & Co. in 1829, there stood a dwelling-house on the premises and a number of skins and a shop were included in the mortgage. In Mr. Jenkins' "Old Quaker Village" we read that "Ebenezer Hallett's house stood on the spot where now stands the house of Reuben K. Farris. It was a low, double house and back of it was a tannery."

April 16, 1831, Moses Burgess, carpenter or "housewright," bought that portion of the above-named tract which now interests us as the proposed library site. At that time, the shop which had belonged to the former owner and tanner, Ebenezer Hallet, was the only building on this land. Mr. Jenkins states that the house "was built by Moses Burgess. He came from West Barnstable, worked at his trade—that of a carpenter—and built for himself this house. Later, he moved back to his old home."

Whether or not Moses Burgess built the house immediately after buying the land in 1831, we have no means of knowing, but we do know that when, in 1846, he deeded to Elizabeth Hawes and Lidia Wood, the present house had been built. Adjoining the premises on the Northerly side was the land of School District No. 7, the "little red schoolhouse" standing thereon until 1855. On the Southerly side, close to the County Road (now Main Street), stood the shoe store of Elisha Jenkins, at that time a long, low building in which, some years before (probably when the tannery was nearby), shoes had been made as well as sold.

Zenas Wood, son of Lidia, occupied the house and after her death in 1860 became, under her will, the owner of her interest in the premises, his wife, Mercy, acquiring by deed in 1861 the interest which had belonged to her mother, Elizabeth Hawes. A few years later, their sons, Orlando and John, came into possession. Orlando passed the latter part of his life there, dying in 1911 at the age of 86—"a notable example," Mr. Jenkins calls him, "of a young-old man." His brother survived him but a few months.

Title passed to the Library Association from the devisees of Louisa L.S. Bagg, to whom the property had been conveyed by the heirs of John Wood.

And so the South Yarmouth Library, after a devious pilgrimage, comes back to the scene of its earlier days, for "just around the corner" on Union Street, a few rods from its present site, it occupied many years ago a small building which stood back of the Peleg P. Akin residence, now a tool house belonging to the home of his daughter, Mrs. George W. Tupper.

Since that evening in February 1869, when a group of public-spirited men and women met at the home of Stephen Wing and formed a library association, the library has found shelter in various places, spending several decades on Bridge Street and about nine years in the Woman's Club Building. Members of the present organization feel that they have found a fitting place for its permanent home and are very grateful for the encouragement and substantial co-operation that have made this possible.

The South Yarmouth Library building is on the National Register of Historic Places, and it is a busy place. In 2019, there were a total of 184,969 visits to the library. Its mission statement:

> *Yarmouth Town Libraries will provide expert assistance and up-to-date information resources broad enough to meet the informational, recreational, and cultural needs of its residents and visitors to the community and to Cape Cod. The public will have access to, and increased awareness of, current topics and titles in multiple formats. Yarmouth Town Libraries will inspire children to become lifelong readers and will support continuous learning for all ages. Yarmouth Town Libraries will offer safe, accessible spaces and opportunities for residents and library users to meet, formally and informally, in a variety of programs for all ages.*

It even has a vision statement:

> *The Yarmouth Town Libraries serve all residents of the community, as they seek facts and ideas for life, as they read for pleasure, as they become informed citizens of a free society, and as they prepare themselves for the future. Skilled library staff members develop collections, provide both local and remote resources, and efficiently manage the library in order to effectively meet the public's needs.*

Well said, well done.

19

WEST DENNIS

WEST DENNIS FREE PUBLIC LIBRARY
260 MAIN STREET (ROUTE 28), WEST DENNIS, MA 02670
508-398-2050
WWW.WESTDENNISLIBRARY.ORG

A great library doesn't have to be big or beautiful. It doesn't have to have the best facilities or the most efficient staff or the most users. A great library provides. It is enmeshed in the life of a community in a way that makes it indispensable.
—Vicki Myron (b. 1947, American author and librarian)

An old dress shop got a new life in 2003 when the books of the next-door West Dennis Free Public Library, in need of much more space, moved in and the dresses moved out.

Built in 1924 to house the library that had been established in 1920, the original one-room structure was expanded in 1961, but the latest change tripled its useable space and created "more of everything…more parking, more reading room, more materials," according to the library website. It's also handicapped accessible, and upstairs are rooms for exhibits and meetings.

Writers' workshops; lectures by historians, artists and authors; an annual Mother's Day Tea; and even a "Read to Puppies" event for children are some of the creative programs at the West Dennis Library. It seems that this

STREET VIEW AND LIBRARY, WEST DENNIS, CAPE COD, MASS.   2A1554

In 1924, the West Dennis Library got its own building (*right*) with a Palladian window. *The Walter "Red" Winn Collection/Nevins Memorial Library, Methuen, Massachusetts.*

library has always had a penchant for fun. In the *Register* of August 28, 1936, a library fundraiser that drew three hundred guests was described:

> *A sum of $250 was realized from the fashion parade and garden party given at the summer home of Mr. and Mrs. Harry F. Doherty for the benefit of West Dennis library. There were 82 entries in the fashion parade, Mrs. Howard F. Sherman with her two young daughters, Constance and Nancy Ann, receiving, the largest number of votes for their unique costumes. They were gowned in complete costumes of the 1800 period. Other entrants were Miss Virginia Hall representing period of 1830; Miss Elaine Cash, 1835; Mrs. Albert L. Gifford, 1840; Mrs. J.E. Montgomery, 1845; Mrs. George L. Wheelock, 1850; Misses Marie Louise Bittner and Mary Lee Williams, 1860; Mrs. Burton Doherty, 1885; Mrs. Lester O'Neil and Miss Danis Erdine O'Neil, 1870; Mrs. Williams, 1880; Mrs. George Swift, 1885; Mrs. Dorothy Newcomb, 1885; Mrs. Alice Perry, 1890; Mrs. Frederick M. Sears, 1890; Miss Cecile Paine, 1895; Miss Jean Perry, 1895; Miss Dythea Rogers, 1895; Miss Mary Lewis Baker, 1900; Mrs. Frank Johnson, 1905; Mrs. Gordon Baker and Miss Marie Rockwell, 1905; Miss Louise Williams, 1910; Miss Eunice Williams, 1910; Miss Anne Sousley, 1910; Mrs. Ireland, 1915; Mrs. William S.*

Ryder, 1915; Mrs. John Heckman, 1925. Music was furnished by Miss Emma Winslow, piano; Samuel R. Small, violin. Bernard M. Sheridan introduced the fashion reviewers. Miss Lucy Wheelock welcomed the 300 guests assembled in the grove at the Doherty home.

That said, it's also a serious library. Along with its regular collection of books and other materials to borrow, the West Dennis Free Public Library also contains part of the town's most precious treasure. In 2009, the Dennis Historical Society's Pauline (Wixon) Derick Library collection was housed in the Josiah Dennis Manse Museum, but the space was not conducive to comfortable research or even just browsing. That November, everything was moved to the second floor of the West Dennis Library, into much more commodious quarters.

In addition to books for finding information about families and historical events, there are photographs to peruse, along with diaries, deeds, scrapbooks and letters related to the town of Dennis and the mid-Cape area.

The maritime collections and genealogical information are extremely popular. The Dennis Historical Society has been gathering and digitizing everything that it's possible to safeguard in this manner for many years.

The West Dennis Library moved just next door, to the right of its 1924 building, in 2003. *Author's collection.*

There are audio copies of interviews with residents long deceased and videos from before 1940. Photograph collections are organized and catalogued by dedicated archivists; these present a unique history of this region from 1845 to today that is, of course, irreplaceable.

It's exciting when people in the photos are finally recognized by a descendant or historian and proper identification can be added to the file. It's also gratifying to see an archival picture of a house that was demolished long ago. The Dennis Historical Commission has put its collection of old house photos on permanent loan to the library so that these images will live on—as will this whimsical blurb from the January 10, 1925 *Register*, which informed its readers that

> the West Dennis library has received a gift of a stuffed alligator from Mr. Andrew H. Baker, proprietor of the St. Petersburg Alligator Farm, Florida. This small member of the saurian family sits erect and is wired to serve as a reading lamp, his front paws holding electric lamp bulbs. Mr. Baker is a former West Dennis boy.

The Baker family is credited with having among them some twenty-nine sea captains. The Ezra Baker School and Baker Park in West Dennis are named for family members. So many lived in the Main Street area that part of West Dennis was known as Baker Town.

20

DENNIS PORT

DENNIS PUBLIC LIBRARY
5 HALL STREET, DENNIS PORT, MA 02639
508-760-6219
WWW.DENNISPUBLICLIBRARY.ORG

*Libraries will get you through times of no money
better than money will get you through times of no libraries.*
—Anne Herbert (1950–2015, American journalist)

Dennis Public Library, just off Route 28 in Dennis Port, is a big, spiffy place with every sort of modern amenity in terms of books, research, movies and music, as well as state-of-the-art technology and plenty of room to expand the collections.

It's the only one of Dennis's five libraries that is funded by the town; the other four are privately run, raising money by themselves (with a little contributed by the town). There was a bit of controversy in the seven or so years before this library was built in 2005, as many residents wanted a modern, central library and others wanted to keep the smaller village libraries. When it was all done, the town of Dennis had five delightful libraries, each special and useful. (The Chase Library in West Harwich is only a quarter mile away, too.)

The mission statement for all the Dennis libraries says it well: "The Dennis Libraries strive to provide current information, titles, and technology

Dennis Public Library opened in 2005 and includes the Cape Cod Genealogical Society Library and Research Room. *Author's collection.*

in welcoming settings and diverse programs that offer affordable learning opportunities and foster multigenerational community interaction." The directors of all the libraries come together frequently to define and discuss how to serve this community; there's no rivalry, only cooperation.

In addition to books, DVDs, audiobooks and periodicals, the library has public access computers, printers and faxing, Chromebooks, laptops and Wi-Fi hotspots to check out. There is even a professional-grade disc cleaner for personal CDs or DVDs, fixing minor scratches and dirt, for a small fee.

The comprehensive research databases of the Massachusetts Library System are available here, along with Encyclopedia Britannica for adults and children.

Patrons can read the *Cape Cod Times*, both current and archival, and the library offers access to the Mango languages app. The Dennis Public Library website has a reliable list of links to find information about health (National Library of Medicine, U.S. National Health Center, Food and Drug Administration, PubMed, Disability Information, Physician's Desk Reference

Online), Massachusetts links, local links (Town of Dennis, Chamber of Commerce, Cape Cod Transit Bus Schedule, Dennis Historical Society), federal links (tax information, legislation, census) and legal information (Barnstable Law Library, Massachusetts legal help).

There's a Cape Cod Collection of nonfiction, fiction and reference books, and the Cape Cod Genealogical Society's Genealogy Room offers hours for the public to get help with research questions. The Cape Cod Salties Sportfishing Club created and donated a nicely curated collection of books and videos to check out for those who need to know where the best fishing spots can be found or how to do specific fishing tasks. The Bayberry Quilters Guild numbers over three hundred members, and they have given a collection of books on their topic to Dennis Public Library. The Echos Culturels Collection fosters the learning of foreign languages for all ages and levels of experience.

Each month, a different artist can exhibit work in the Benjamin and Ruth Muse Meeting Room. Children enjoy story hours, craft projects and story walks, and there are book discussion groups for adults. Museum passes for reduced admission (a few are free, check first) are available for the Cahoon Museum of American Art, Cotuit; Cape Cod Museum of Art, Dennis; Heritage Museums and Gardens, Sandwich; John F. Kennedy Hyannis Museum; Massachusetts Parks, multiple locations; provides free parking (admission) to the Massachusetts Department of Conservation and Recreation Parks, including South Cape Beach, Horseneck Beach and Nickerson State Park, if your car has a Massachusetts license plate; Museum of Fine Arts, Boston; Museum of Science, Boston; Mystic Aquarium, Mystic, Connecticut; Pilgrim Monument and Provincetown Museum; Sandwich Glass Museum; Whydah Pirate Museum, West Yarmouth; and Zoo New England, Stoneham and Boston.

21

SOUTH DENNIS

South Dennis Free Public Library
389 Main Street, South Dennis, MA 02660
508-394-8954
www.SouthDennisLibrary.org

My real education, the superstructure, the details, the true architecture, I got out of the public library. For an impoverished child whose family could not afford to buy books, the library was the open door to wonder and achievement, and I can never be sufficiently grateful that I had the wit to charge through that door and make the most of it. Now, when I read constantly about the way in which library funds are being cut and cut, I can only think that the door is closing and that American society has found one more way to destroy itself.
—Isaac Asimov (1920–1992, American author)

A Victorian dollhouse nestled in a thicket, the South Dennis Free Public Library can be described with one perfect word: darling. Steep gables, pointy shutters and genuine gingerbread trim have made this a must-see attraction for local, national and international visitors to the Mid-Cape area for decades. Artists and photographers flock to the site—if they don't drive right by it—to capture a beautiful example of American Gothic architecture with the bonus of being filled with more than fifteen thousand books, DVDs, puzzles and games.

The most fanciful library on Cape Cod is hiding in plain sight in South Dennis. *Author's collection.*

Starting life as the home of seafarer John Rose (who was also the first Portuguese citizen of Dennis) in 1856, it was later a cobbler's shop, then the home of "Emily Smalle, the reputed ardent poetess of South Dennis" according to the library's website; finally, sea captain Jonathan Matthews bequeathed it to the town to use as a library in 1926. The newly incorporated South Dennis Free Public Library Association began running the enterprise in 1928 with some financial assistance from the town and continues to do so to this day.

Electricity was installed in 1950, and the pot-bellied stove provided the only heat for eight years after that; the librarian was charged with poking up the embers during the short time the building was open for patrons each week.

When the tiny library's popularity outpaced its footprint, much care was taken to expand the space while respecting its unique architecture. Colonial Williamsburg restoration expert Gordon Robb was hired in the 1960s to design an addition that featured harmonious quatrefoils (think four leaf clovers) and fancy dentil work. This is one library that didn't suffer a tasteless "moderne" makeover.

The only nod to the twenty-first century is the excellent collection of materials like STEM (science, technology, engineering, and mathematics) activity kits for youngsters, along with high-speed internet and wireless access, of course. The librarians are particularly eager to help; they live up to their motto: "Our mission is to make sure that nobody leaves empty-handed."

22

DENNIS

DENNIS MEMORIAL LIBRARY
1020 OLD BASS RIVER ROAD, DENNIS, MA 02638
508-385-2255
WWW.DENNISMEMORIALLIBRARY.ORG

The library is the temple of learning,
and learning has liberated more people than all the wars in history.
—Carl Thomas Rowan (1925–2000, American journalist)

Named in honor of the Dennis residents who fought and died in World War I, Dennis Memorial Library has been the village's fond friend since 1924.

It has been expanded many times over the past one hundred years, enabling book collections, DVDs, periodicals and the children's section to grow along with the population. The most recent addition was a 3,600-square-foot space to integrate more technology into library offerings.

Its specialty is a variety of materials for patrons with vision problems, such as audio-described movies. There is a Dell computer with a large screen monitor and magnifier with Zoom Text; a Dell computer with a JAWS screen reader and Kurzweil software (so the computer talks to you); Perkins "Talking Books" recorder and tapes; more than one thousand regular tape cassette audiobooks and over five hundred CD audio books; an Optelec magnifier; Low Vision Resource catalogues and information; and tutoring on internet browsing, e-mail and other programs.

Dennis Memorial Library was named in honor of those who died in World War I. *Author's collection.*

History buffs will appreciate the library's nonfiction titles on Cape Cod history as well as fiction by Joseph C. Lincoln, Phoebe Atwood Taylor and Gladys Taber. Information on lighthouses, Cape Cod architecture and flora and fauna unique to the Cape Cod region is available too.

Dennis Memorial Library offers English as a Second Language classes, homework help, craft groups, book clubs, notary public and programs for children. The town has a rich history.

Europeans settled here in 1639 when Dennis was called the East Precinct part of Yarmouth; on incorporation in 1793, the area was named for the pastor of the Dennis Union Church, Josiah Dennis.

The Native Americans were here long before that, of course, and the Town of Dennis chose to behave with dignity toward a cemetery where a number of Nobscussett were buried. In 1828, the town fenced in the area and erected a marker: "Burial Ground of the Nobscussett Tribe of Indians, of Which Tribe Mashantampaine was Chief." It's about a mile east from the library along Route 6A and can be found by walking down a hedgerow path directly across the road from Osprey Lane; it is tradition to behave with reverence and bring a small offering of a natural item (such as a feather or shell) of personal spiritual significance and leave it on the stone bench. These people were the town's true "firstcomers."

Numerous fundraisers for the library have been held over the past century. The front page of *The Register* on August 11, 1923, described one:

> *The dance last Friday evening held for the benefit of the Dennis Memorial library was a wonderful success. Everyone enjoyed a delightful evening. Mrs. J.D. Anderson and Miss Margaret Anderson of Springfield and Mrs. Jeannette Peto and Mrs. Henrietta Trusty of New York City deserve a great deal of credit for their untiring efforts in making the ball such a success. Mr. Baker and his variety orchestra of five pieces also deserve a special mention for the way in which they arranged the program of music for the evening. Mr. Baker showed his versatility and musical abilities in the manner in which he put over the latest song hits, and featured a new musical success, "Oh, You Little Sun-uv-er-gun," written by Joseph Solman, pianist, now playing with Scotti Holmes, the original dancing bass-player, and his famous orchestra at Bournehurst-on-the-Canal. The stage was beautifully decorated by Mr. F.R. Zwicker, art director and publicity manager of Bournehurst, and Mr. J.D. Anderson, Jr., of the Blue Door Flower Shoppe, Woonsocket, RI. The dance was in the nature of a Mardi gras, confetti, streamers, noisemakers, and novelties putting a realistic atmosphere to the ball. The surrounding towns did more than their share, while in Dennis itself the support was slow in getting underway. It is being considered holding a few more affairs with extraordinary attractions never before shown in this locality. It is hoped that Dennis will co-operate fully in making the dances even better successes in the future. This is only the beginning. Let's all get together and reach that $5,000 mark as soon as possible. Watch for the announcements for the next affair, which will surpass this last brilliant party. When the time comes let everybody say, "Let's Go!"*

EAST DENNIS

JACOB SEARS MEMORIAL LIBRARY
23 CENTER STREET, EAST DENNIS, MA 02641
508-385-8151
WWW.JACOBSEARSLIBRARY.ORG

The best of my education has come from the public library.....My tuition fee is a bus fare and once in a while, five cents a day for an overdue book. You don't need to know very much to start with, if you know the way to the public library.
—*Lesley Conger (Shirley Suttles, 1922–2010, American author)*

Tucked away on a side street in Quivet Neck—a physically tiny but historically significant section of the small village of East Dennis—is the magnificent Jacob Sears Library, the best of all secret Cape Cod libraries for its ability to hide in plain sight.

And what a sight it is. When it was designed in 1895, the architecture was appropriately called Modified French Chateau, which is exactly what it looks like with its multiple turrets and pointy dormers over long windows, but nowadays this is referred to as Shingle Style, a wholly American invention with a supercilious definition:

> *The style conveyed a sense of the house as continuous volume. This effect—of the building as an envelope of space, rather than a great mass, was enhanced by the visual tautness of the flat shingled surfaces, the*

horizontal shape of many Shingle Style houses, and the emphasis on horizontal continuity, both in exterior details and in the flow of spaces within the houses.

That being dutifully said, the library looks like a beautiful little chateau. Inside, all the woodwork, ceiling, roof trusses and fireplace mantel are made of mahogany; the main room doubles as a meeting hall when the bookshelves are rolled away. A stage with velvet curtains faces a balcony overlooking everything.

In her 1962 autobiography *The Lonely Life*, actress Bette Davis (1908–1989) mentioned performing on this very stage. She had come to Dennis in the hopes of acting at the Cape Playhouse, exactly three miles away. She did get a job there—as an usher—but later in that summer of 1928 Davis was offered a role with the Junior Players in *The Charm School*, presented at the Jacob Sears Memorial Hall (library). "It was a benefit performance for the Methodist Church," she wrote. "We were such a success that we were invited to play in three or four nearby towns."

One reading room has a bay window and a fireplace with tiles depicting some of the eight colossal clipper ships that were built in Shiverick Shipyard (no longer in existence) in East Dennis: the *Hippogriffe* in 1851, the *Belle of the*

The Jacob Sears Memorial Library is an exquisite surprise in East Dennis. *Dennis Historical Society Archives.*

West in 1853, the *Christopher Hall* in 1858. A recently refurbished portrait of Jacob Sears in a gleaming gold frame hangs above.

The backyard Wi-Fi Garden is a nod to the twenty-first century, along with a few computers for patrons to use, but it is commendable that the Jacob Sears Library hasn't been ruined with aggressive upgrades. It is perfect as it is. Plus, it's safely listed on the National Register of Historic Places now.

Two previous library incarnations lived before the purpose-built edifice on Center Street: William F. Howes developed a library association in private homes from 1866 to 1870; when Nathaniel Myrick and Captain Prince S. Crowell each made donations of about $500, the library was able to move to Worden Hall on the Old King's Highway and its collection expanded to well over one thousand volumes. Circulation was for members who paid $0.50 per year to borrow books.

Jacob Sears was born in 1823 and made a fortune in the cranberry business. Not only did he own twenty-eight bogs, but he also developed a way to ship the cranberries in water-filled casks so they would stay fresh and undamaged during long voyages. By the time he died at age forty-seven, he was a successful businessman in numerous endeavors.

Sears had fond memories of attending the East Dennis School on the corner of Center and School Streets, and he was disappointed when the fourteen one-room schoolhouses in the town of Dennis were, per state mandate, replaced with five public schools (one in each village) in the 1860s. He did not believe that children could receive a well-rounded education in these new modern schools, so he left money in his will for a library to be built in conjunction with a meeting hall so that musical events, lectures and other forms of auxiliary educational experiences could be offered.

Sears's will stated that following the death of his wife, Olive, his estate should be used "for the benefit of the inhabitants of East Dennis and vicinity, for educational purposes" on Quivet Neck.

Jacob died in 1871 and Olive in 1892. Jacob's siblings contested the will in a case that went to the Massachusetts Supreme Judicial Court in 1893. Oliver Wendell Holmes Jr. was serving as an associate justice and ruled that the Sears will "constitutes a good gift to charity and may be executed as a valid charitable trust." The court also formulated a process to carry out and administer the intent set forth in the will:

> *One-third part of the said trust property, as near as may be, shall be appropriated and used for the purchase of a tract of land the erection of a building and appurtenances thereon, to be located upon said Quivet Neck.*

Inside the Jacob Sears Memorial Library is a fancy stage with velvet curtains where Bette Davis performed. *Author's collection.*

> *Said building shall be provide with a suitable hall fitted and adopted for the giving of lectures, and with suitable rooms fitted and adopted for the maintaining of a library.*

Use of the facility was to be free for all. The formal dedication of the building occurred on July 10, 1896.

PART III

•

The Lower Cape

24

WEST HARWICH

CHASE LIBRARY
7 ROUTE 28, WEST HARWICH, MA 02671
508-432-2610
WWW.CHASE-LIBRARY.COM

Nothing is pleasanter than exploring a library.
—Walter Savage Landor (1775–1864, English writer and poet)

At a very busy intersection on the busiest route on Cape Cod there's a roadside haven: a charming wee library where, crossing over the threshold, the traffic noises subside and visitors slide into a welcome hush.

The first thing you see is a large oil painting over the fireplace. (Or, if you're from someplace where libraries don't usually have fireplaces, you might notice the carved wooden mantelpiece and logs beneath it.) In the portrait of co-founder Salome Chase, painted in 1897 by F.D. Henwood, she's wearing a gown that she also wore to Queen Victoria's Golden Jubilee in 1887. The whole thing makes an attractive tableau.

The Chase Library sprang from the cheerful positivity of its founders, Ruth Nickerson (who was married to Dr. John P. Nickerson) and Chase; both saw the need for a reading room and, after garnering books for two years, began one in the living room of Nickerson's home. They called it the Sunshine Club and encouraged "a little band of children" to contribute their efforts in forming a library.

Still as winsome and earnest as ever, Chase Library is a must-visit. *Author's collection.*

When the popularity of the enterprise outstripped its available space, Salome and her husband, Colonel Caleb Chase, donated a house for the library association to sell and use the profits to build the present library.

The last-born of Job Chase's seventeen children, Caleb had eschewed the family fishing tradition for a career in business. Colonel Chase's portrait may be seen on every can of Chase and Sanborn Coffee, as, at the age of thirty-one, he joined forces with James Sanborn in 1862 to create the lucrative company. It became the first coffee firm in the world to pack and ship roasted ground coffee in sealed cans. Before this revolutionary process, customers bought coffee beans in bulk, and their quality deteriorated too quickly. Canned coffee stayed fresh longer. Colonel Chase eventually owned vast coffee plantations all over the world; he earned his reputation for generosity by sharing his wealth to help the poor on Cape Cod and beyond.

He and Salome lived on Beacon Street in Boston but spent summers in their West Harwich home, Good Cheer. When the much-appreciated philanthropist died in 1908, scores of devotees accompanied his coffin the nearly one hundred miles by train to Pine Grove Cemetery, West Harwich, for burial.

Shortly afterward, Dr. and Mrs. Nickerson contributed a corner of their own land, an apple orchard, and construction began on the new Chase Library.

All walls, the mantel and bookcases are cypress wood; the ceilings are embossed steel, and the floors are polished maple. The cost to build it was $1,771. In addition, a Miller piano was presented by the "summer people." The library is a combination of Craftsman and Shingle Style architecture, though the identifying Shingle features of eyebrow dormer windows and a large porch with shingled knee walls are no longer part of the building; the porch was removed in 1974. However, most of its original work is intact, so Chase Library is on the National Register of Historic Places.

The first librarian was Ruth Nickerson (1868–1948); she was involved in many local organizations, including the Harwich Women's Club and Ladies Circle of the West Harwich Baptist Church, but she dedicated her time and energy to Chase Library, where she was active as a director for thirty years. Amazingly, the next librarian, Mary Hentz, held the position for sixty-four years.

Nowadays, this library doesn't demand that you present a library card because it doesn't use them. And all the books are listed in a wonderfully old-fashioned card catalogue. It does offer delivery to homebound people, along with curbside delivery, and there are always books for sale when the library is open (two days each week). Even with its small size and minimal hours, it has over fifteen thousand materials and an annual circulation of more than six thousand. Kids will love the Children's Corner in the back room, where big teddy bears sit on rocking chairs, waiting for a story.

With a nickname like "The Little Library that Could" and the staff's permanent invitation to "Come in for a cookie and a smile," it's fun to spend some time here.

25

HARWICH PORT

Harwich Port Library
49 Bank Street, Harwich Port, MA 02645
508-432-3320
(No website)

The public library is where place and possibility meet.
—Stuart Dybek (b. 1942, American author)

A French marquis was a major donor to the Harwich Port Library's building fund in 1923. The Marquis de Sers was a good friend of Anne Van Buren, the woman who spearheaded bringing a library to the village; she had already contributed five hundred books, so all that was needed was a place to shelve them.

The marquis gave $1,000—worth at least sixteen times that today—and Mrs. Paul Gray, a summer resident from Detroit, donated the land on Bank Street. Gideon Freeman gave another $1,000 for the construction, and soon the new library was complete. It was fully chartered as a public library that same year, operated by the Harwich Port Library Association, and began receiving a town subsidy in 1926.

Not just a library, the building also comprises a large community room that, over the past one hundred years, has hosted events like suppers and dances, Red Cross meetings, gatherings of Girl Scouts, recitals, concerts and tea parties. In the August 1, 1927 issue of *Cape Cod Magazine*, it was described by Talmadge Fletcher:

There is the large hall, capable of holding very sizeable functions, with its equipped stage and modern heating arrangement…a dainty kitchen, with curtains of a delightful apricot shade, dainty dishes in any quantity, and every device, it would seem, of an up-to-date home kitchen. The dishes are not plain white and "serviceable," which means thick and uninviting, but are of pretty colored patterns that attract.…How many towns lack a community house, and what a lack it is you realize once you see one in operation.

Harwich Port Library is delightfully traditional, with no website and no computers; the small house has all sorts of tiny and curiously shaped cupboards with wrought-iron latches, along with three fireplaces and a real wooden card catalogue. The sunny children's room has little tables

Harwich Port Library looks small from the street but has three fireplaces and a community hall. *Author's collection.*

and chairs and a huge collection of colorful books; story times are held here—sweet, simple and fun.

The annual meeting of the Cape Cod Library Club met in Harwich Port in 1935. Each year, a different location hosted the much-anticipated event, to which all librarians in the counties of Barnstable, Dukes (Martha's Vineyard) and Nantucket were invited. From the October 24, 1935 *Falmouth Enterprise*:

> *The Cape Cod Library Club is holding its annual meeting on Thursday and Friday of this week, at Melrose Inn, Harwich Port. Today the morning meeting was a business meeting, with introductory remarks by Mrs. Edwin P. Goss, vice-president of the Harwich Port Library Association. Mrs. Charles Eldredge, of the Sagamore information booth, was speaker at the afternoon session....A tea at the Harwich Port library, and sightseeing trips, will complete the first day's program. On Friday morning a roll call of librarian members asks a report from every member with comment on books read during the past year. An afternoon meeting is to have a speaker not yet announced. Miss Cecelia L. Bowerman, Falmouth librarian, is secretary of the club. She is attending the sessions today and tomorrow. The library will be open as usual with a substitute in charge.*

The club was started in 1900 by Mabel Simpkins of Sandyside in Yarmouth Port (later referred to as Mrs. George Agassiz of Boston); she was a member of the Massachusetts Library Commission, which encouraged the formation of local library clubs. Librarians could compare notes about the challenges they faced, successes they counted and new ways to engage young people in enjoying all that libraries have to offer—if this is even possible. Consider what *Cape Cod Library Club History 1900–1950* stated:

> *In 1903 Miss Abby Sargent advocated having other things besides books, such as pictures, which will prove attractive to boys and girls and influence them to go to the library instead of spending time at the corner grocery or on the curbstones.*

To which its compiler, librarian Caroline R. Siebens, commented in 1950, "No movies, radio, or television then, but still the problem of the juvenile and adolescent." We in the twenty-first century can only sigh.

26

HARWICH

BROOKS FREE LIBRARY
739 MAIN STREET, HARWICH, MA 02645
508-430-7562
WWW.BROOKSFREELIBRARY.ORG

Whatever the cost of our libraries,
the price is cheap compared to that of an ignorant nation.
—Walter Cronkite (1916–2009, American broadcast journalist, in American
Library Association "Libraries Change Lives" Campaign, 1995)

Big, bright and cheerful, Brooks Free Library's mission statement matches its physicality: "The library will promote full and equal access to information and ideas, the love of reading, the joy of learning, and engagement with the arts, sciences and humanities."

The library was named for Henry Cobb Brooks, whose great-great-grandfather Beriah Broadbrooks made his home in Harwich the very year it was incorporated (1694). Henry's father, Obed, had their surname legally changed to Brooks in 1806, and various family members lent their name and efforts to numerous civic endeavors: Brooks Park, Brooks Academy, the Brooks Block and of course Brooks Free Library. Henry was a successful shipbuilder in Boston and operated a sailing line to Australia, and his siblings back home in Harwich started banks, a school and several shops. When he

Brooks Free Public Library in Harwich is a city block full of books. *Author's collection.*

built the huge Brooks Block building in 1880, the east side of the second floor was for Brooks Free Library, along with milliners and dressmakers; downstairs there were shops for dry goods and furniture, curtains and wallpapers and parlor stoves.

The Second District Court of Barnstable operated on the ground floor of the Brooks Block from 1936 until 1970; the judge's bench was left behind and is now a grand addition to the reference area, complete with the official gavel. Next to it is another item of furniture that didn't leave the building: an antique Borne Settee, often called a round lobby sofa, which had to stay upstairs because it's too unwieldy to fit through the doors.

When the library opened to the public on New Year's Day in 1881, Henry's sister Tamesin was the librarian; she held the position for ten years, unpaid. By 1897, the new librarian was earning twelve and a half cents per hour. The doors were open to patrons only on Saturday afternoons. Now Brooks Library is open about forty-eight hours every week.

In June 1881, Pliny Nickerson of Harwich donated forty Rogers Groups Statues to the library. The thought-provoking plaster works by nineteenth-century artist John Rogers depict American vignettes such as women working a spinning wheel, weary Civil War soldiers and *Playing Checkers Up at the Farm*, plus several Shakespearean scenes. They are reminiscent of Norman Rockwell images but in sculpture form. There's also a lineup of plaster busts from the library's opening reception on Thanksgiving Day 1880 of Shakespeare, Milton, Byron, Burns, Dickens and Washington Irving, which can be seen today in the second-floor reference area.

One hundred years later, the library needed more space for its diverse collection of books, which had grown steadily through the decades. It was time for expansion.

Librarian Suzanne Martell decorated an antique round settee with books; it's next to the vintage judge's bench in Brooks Library. *Author's collection.*

It's not every day that voters get behind an expensive library renovation project, but in 1996, Harwich Town Meeting gave unanimous support to the idea, followed by 65 percent of residents voting to spend over $3 million on expanding and improving the library. (Later, a $1.3 million federal Library Services and Technology Act construction grant was received from the Massachusetts Board of Library Commissioners, reducing taxpayer cost to $1.8 million.) The Friends of Brooks Library contributed money to buy the adjacent lot on Bank Street for additional parking, to create a basement meeting room and to provide furnishings for the renovated facility. The completed project won an award from the Massachusetts Historical Commission for successfully maintaining the historic character of the building.

Of course, a library isn't just a building. Thoughtful librarians affect the place as much as, or more than, functional infrastructure. For instance, what if you needed information on a subject but you were too uncomfortable to check out a book about it? Yes, Massachusetts state law protects your confidentiality, and librarians do uphold this standard as well, but sometimes patrons feel too vulnerable to risk it. Enter the "Confidential Corner" at Brooks Library. In a quiet area upstairs, there are shelves of books about addiction, alcoholism, gender identity, mental health, suicide and sexual abuse. These books may be borrowed and returned without any official record. Brooks Library simply trusts that people who use this service will indeed bring the books back for the next person who needs them. And they do.

Here's a fantastic example of what a library can be and do for the community, if the right people are at the helm. In the summer of 2019, a tornado touched down in Harwich, ripping up trees and knocking out power to much of the town. Fortunately, the town had voted to install a generator some time before, so Brooks Library still had electricity. When the staff heard the tornado warnings, they calmly gathered all the patrons into the basement meeting room, invited those in the parking lot to join them and engaged the kids in fun activities. It's a testament to the librarians' professionalism that the children never had a clue that anything unusual was going on outside.

In the following days, the library remained open for additional hours as residents needed to use the internet, charge their devices and get accurate information about what had happened and when power would be restored.

They gathered to talk, do jigsaw puzzles, take out books and share their experiences—as well as express gratitude that their library welcomed everyone in to provide a much-needed sense of community and continuity.

27

BREWSTER

BREWSTER

BREWSTER LADIES LIBRARY
1822 MAIN STREET (ROUTE 6A), BREWSTER, MA 02631
508-896-3913
WWW.BREWSTERLADIESLIBRARY.ORG

The only thing that you absolutely have to know, is the location of the library.
—Albert Einstein (1879–1955, theoretical physicist)

Yes, gentlemen are allowed. The name reflects how the library started, not how it was meant to go on. In 1852, Sarah Augusta Mayo and Mary Louise Cobb gathered ten more friends to start a subscription library. Each person would pay for membership, thereby funding book-buying and allowing members to borrow books. The first location was in the home of Sarah's father, Captain Mayo, at 1772 Main Street. When the library opened to the public in early 1853, men were welcome to borrow any of the two hundred books—but at a higher price than ladies.

Nowadays, gender plays no role in the library/patron process. In fact, after some clamor during the 1970s about the "Ladies" designation and the possible confusion over male exclusion, it was put to a vote at the annual library meeting: keep the name historical, or change it? The name stayed, obviously, but in the 1990s a little something extra was added: "Your Community Library."

By the 1860s, there was no more space for books in Captain Mayo's house, so another seafarer, Captain Joseph Nickerson, donated $1,000 to a fledgling fund to construct a dedicated library building. The original design, says the library's website, featured "two comfortable parlors, each with a fireplace" and both rooms were lined with shelves for the collection.

The library is a good example of Stick Style architecture, in which narrow planks, or sticks, are laid over the exterior as a pure decoration. It was popular in the designs of train stations as well as other public buildings of the era.

Through many decades of additions and department rearrangement, the Brewster Ladies Library has grown exponentially in materials (56,000) and scope (circulation is well over 180,000 per year). Every month there's a new art show.

The Library of Things to check out here includes an electronics tool kit ("Contains all the poking, prying, gripping, lifting, ESD safety, and screw driving tools needed to service consumer electronics") and a thirty-nine-piece general repair hand tool set; a metal detector; badminton and volleyball set; binoculars; Wi-Fi hotspots; and board games.

Its Memory Support Collection features books, guides, activities, music, videos and other resources for those suffering from memory loss, as well as help for their caregivers.

Strolling in front of Brewster Ladies Library circa 1900. *Caro A. Dugan Collection of the Brewster Historical Society.*

The number of resources through the Brewster Ladies Library is impressive. Available by visiting the library's website are the Barnstable County Department of Human Services Directory; Boston Public Library Free Online Resources; Cape Cod Native Plants, an online tool to find the native plants best suited for specific sites in terms of ecological function and benefit; FindHelp, a community portal that provides residents of Cape Cod online access to available resources such as housing, healthcare and early education; *Consumer Reports*; HeritageQuest, a database to find ancestors using the U.S. Census 1790–1930, locate people and places with Persi, a database of 1.6 million genealogy and local history articles, and even search selected records from the Revolutionary War. With Libby, patrons can get free e-books, audiobooks, magazines and video on a computer or smartphone. By using the library's subscription to Hoopla, card holders can download the free Hoopla digital mobile app on their Android or IOS device or access it via their Roku player or at hoopladigital.com, to get movies, music and books.

And, finally, read the *Cape Cod Times* for free, along with the *New York Times* and *The Register*, through the library's website. Youngsters will enjoy Digital Escape Rooms there, too.

Museum passes can be reserved online. Free admission is available for the Brewster Historical Society/Cobb House at 739 Lower Road in Brewster, Cape Cod Museum of Art in Dennis, the Sandwich Glass Museum, any state park in Massachusetts for a car registered in Massachusetts and the USS Constitution Museum in Charlestown Navy Yard. Admission is five dollars per person for the Isabella Stewart Gardner Museum in Boston and the Institute of Contemporary Art in Boston. Half-price admission is available for the Museum of Science in Boston, the Cape Cod Children's Museum in Mashpee, the Edward Gorey House in Yarmouth Port, the Boston Children's Museum and New England Aquarium in Boston.

According to the 1899 Report of the Free Massachusetts Library Commission,

> *In 1878 the* [Brewster Ladies Library] *was legally incorporated in the town of Brewster. From that time until the present it has been maintained from the proceeds of entertainments which the ladies have gotten up and from the income derived from subscribers. Last December* [1897] *a special meeting was held to discuss the plan of making the library a free one if the cost of maintenance could be secured. Capt. J. Henry Sears offered to give a sum for the ensuing year equal to that derived from subscriptions,*

loan of books, fines, etc. The town voted to pay the salary of the librarian. The town's appropriation for librarian's salary is $50. It was voted to have the library open two days instead of one during every week, as has been the usual practice....Before the library was made free the number of subscribers did not exceed 25, and about fifteen volumes were loaned weekly. Since January 1898, 144 cards have been issued to borrowers, and the loans are from 50 to 60 volumes weekly. Population, 1895: 901; volumes, 1898: 2,700; circulation, about 2,600. The ladies agreed to make the experiment for one year, and, if it should prove a success, to make it a free library permanently.

Apparently, it worked.

28

SOUTH CHATHAM

South Chatham Library
2960 Main Street, South Chatham, MA 02659
508-430-7989
(No website)

To ask why we need libraries at all, when there is so much information available elsewhere, is about as sensible as asking if roadmaps are necessary now that there are so very many roads.
—Jon Bing (1944–2014, Norwegian writer and law professor at the Norwegian Research Center for Computers and Law)

A treasured holdout on the ultramodern world, South Chatham Library is a favorite place for what it is and what it isn't. There's not one computer in the miniature building; the books have paper flaps on the inside back page for borrowers to sign their name when taking out one of the four thousand novels or nonfiction selections.

No one is shushed if they discuss a new author or the latest news around town. Indeed, the librarian understands that part of the little library's appeal is meeting up with neighbors or summer visitors during the two days each week the building is open.

There's a small metal index card box on the desk filled with patrons' names—no one has to carry a library card or barcode. The system works well because one look at this cute, trusting library and anyone who is good at heart would never fail to return a book.

South Chatham Library's clever use of space allows for thousands of books in a small house. *Author's collection.*

Fundraising takes place in the summer, with book sales of the weeded-out items making room for new volumes; shelf space is at a premium, of course, and the regular customers have probably already read everything in the whole library. They all come back anyway, to check out the new books section and have a nice chat.

South Chatham Library is a tough little thing; it has a history of overcoming challenges and always succeeding. It began in 1874 as a shelf of books in a store on Deep Hole Wharf (at the end of Deep Hole Road) operated by Levi Eldridge, who was also an early president of the Cape Cod Five Cents Savings Bank. His daughter Mercelia oversaw the collection. Ten years later, it was called the Pilgrim Library and its 515 books were housed in a Main Street building in which the post office also had space.

The library was definitely becoming an important part of the town, as evidenced by the notations of its new recording secretary, whose job was made all the more official by the library association voting to spend up to $0.75 on a book in which she could record the proceedings of meetings. At the same meeting in 1885, the seven members decided how much the librarian's annual salary would be ($7.00). Book-borrowing was by subscription of $1.00 per year (though this would decrease to $0.50 in 1893), and fundraising efforts such as bean suppers or an evening of entertainment might bring in $5.00 or $6.00. It was a struggle to buy books, repair old ones and keep up with routine expenses, yet the Pilgrim Library persevered.

In 1899, the name was changed to South Chatham Library to avoid confusion with the Pilgrim Library in Truro, and in the following thirty years the collection grew along with library association membership, making many moves from shops to halls and back again. When the Methodist Church (now the South Chatham Community Church) offered in 1933 to lease a bit of their land on which a permanent library could be built, the plan was quickly realized and South Chatham Library has never moved since. Extremely dedicated and creative library association members, directors, librarians and patrons have pursued donations and grants throughout the decades to keep the building warm or cool, in good repair, nicely landscaped and full of books, along with its highly valued sense of community.

29

CHATHAM

ELDREDGE PUBLIC LIBRARY
564 MAIN STREET, CHATHAM, MA 02633
508-945-5170
WWW.ELDREDGELIBRARY.ORG

The richest person in the world—in fact all the riches in the world—couldn't
provide you with anything like the endless, incredible loot
available at your local library.
—Malcolm Forbes (1919–1990, American entrepreneur)

*I*t's ever so much fun to go inside a little castle—and you get to borrow books here, too. Arching eyebrow windows peer out onto Main Street in Chatham from the roof of Eldredge Public Library, a Renaissance/ Romanesque Revival building constructed of Massachusetts materials: West Barnstable brick, Quincy granite and Longmeadow brownstone.

A gift of Chatham native Marcellus Eldredge, the $30,000 building was dedicated on Independence Day in 1896 on a plot of land that cost $1,000. He was born in Chatham and made his fortune in New Hampshire, in banking and especially in brewing. In her excellent 1996 book *A Beacon for Chatham*, Josephine Ives recounted,

> *An apocryphal story, still often repeated in Chatham, suggests that at first*
> *the Town Fathers actually refused it; some people, it seemed, were troubled*
> *that the library had been built with "tainted money," i.e., profits from*

the production and sale of alcoholic beverage. Not until it became known that the Methodist Church across the street had enthusiastically welcomed Marcellus Eldredge's contributions to their building renovation did the Town hastily indicate acceptance. Meanwhile [Mr. Eldredge]…*is said to have commented, "If the Town doesn't want the library, it can come down faster than it went up."*

Fortunately, the town welcomed the gift, thereby bypassing the somewhat controversial possibility of applying for a free Carnegie library. In 1902, Cape Cod Library Club president Charles F. Swift congratulated Chatham for not being indebted to Andrew Carnegie "nor to any other foreign resident, but to the thoughtfulness and kindly interest of their kindred who have gone out from among us, made their impress on the business world, and have remembered the old friends and the old home by their splendid benefactions."

During that same convention of the Cape Cod Library Club in 1902, *The Register* wrote,

Thirty members on the arrival of the train in Chatham were met by a delegation from the officers of the Eldredge Library, who cordially welcomed the visitors and provided barges by which they were conveyed

The roof is looking at you: Eldredge Library in Chatham is Renaissance/Romanesque Revival style (1885). *The Walter "Red" Winn Collection/Nevins Memorial Library, Methuen, Massachusetts.*

to various localities in that delightfully picturesque old town, winding up their peregrinations by a stop at the high land near the lighthouses and ascending the towers of the lights, from which an unrivalled view was obtained. As the ocean was in a rather turbulent mood, the interest in the spectacle was enhanced.

The architect responsible for the beautiful design of Eldredge Library is Albion Marble (a student of H.H. Richardson, who popularized those quirky windows in the United States). Inside are an Italian marble mosaic as well as a magnificent carved oak fireplace mantel. Everywhere are heavy oak doors, wainscoting, shelving and balustrades gleaming with the polish of 125 years. An antique Barber & Huddersfield grandfather clock given by the Hammerstein family stands sentinel. Two stained-glass windows honor sixteenth-century Italian book printers and publishers Lucantonio Giunta and Aldus Manutius, whose creativity and business acumen transformed the industry hundreds of years ago. No wonder Eldredge Library is on the National Register of Historic Places.

The building has endured peacefully enough, but there was a little drama inside the staff room way back in the 1930s to the '50s. When a niece of Marcellus Eldredge came to power as the library's corporator, director, board president *and* treasurer in 1936, she made some unpopular policies; she gave herself sole discretion on what books to buy for the library, for instance, forbidding input even from the librarian who had worked there for twenty-five years and knew what the patrons liked. Board meetings were rarely held, a bevy of disastrous investments drained the coffers and by 1948 circulation had fallen to its lowest level in fifty years. Residents had felt the unpleasant atmosphere at Eldredge Library and tried to save their precious town resource, but the Library Board did nothing. Two groups, the Chatham Woman's Club and the Chamber of Commerce, put up a fight. They got a special article placed on the warrant for the 1950 Town Meeting: funding for "painting, repairing, and general improvement of the Eldredge Public Library building." It passed unanimously, which sent a frosty message to the regime. Soon there was a Citizens Committee to oversee the dispersal of the funds and suggest long-overdue improvements, and all at once the dictatorship moved toward democracy and the library began to flourish. It has since blossomed into a much-loved civic institution in Chatham and beyond.

The ambience now in the main part of Eldredge Public Library is of dignified well-being. It's fortunate that the thick wooden doors have power-

The reading room is filled with stained glass, polished wood and natural light on Main Street in Chatham. *Author's collection.*

assist mechanisms, because they seem as heavy as real castle doors. It's a lovely way to keep the old style relevant. No doubt there are a few quick remodeling tasks that could be undertaken to expedite maintenance, but that would be tragic.

The Children's Room is full of creativity and fun. The ceiling tiles sport scenes hand-painted by youngsters, and vibrant displays of themed books invite kids to explore.

The efforts of the Friends of the Eldredge Public Library each year also continue to translate into vast benefits for patrons; in addition to supplying volunteers to mend frayed books, decorate for holidays and seasons and arrange for programs and classes, the group runs a year-round book sale and funds huge projects like painting the whole interior of the library and buying multiple new laptop computers. Circulation for the first full year of library operations in 1896–97 totaled 11,738 for a population of about 1,800. Pre-COVID numbers (2019) recorded 149,000 visits to the library, and the population was 6,000. The library offered 700 programs, and circulation was 86,000. Marcellus Eldredge would be happy to know that his investment was more than just of a building.

30

ORLEANS

Snow Library
67 Main Street, Orleans, MA 02653
508-240-3760
www.SnowLibrary.org

Public libraries have been a mainstay of my life. They represent an individual's right to acquire knowledge; they are the sinews that bind civilized societies the world over. Without libraries, I would be a pauper, intellectually and spiritually.
—James A. Michener (1907–1997, American author)

Before an electrical fire burned it to the ground during a dreadful blizzard in 1952, Snow Library in Orleans was a fantastic 1877 example of Tudor Revival architecture (though it's been described various ways—Old English, Victorian or English Gothic). Along with the beautiful building, lost was a parchment copy of the act of incorporation of Orleans that was signed by Massachusetts governor John Adams in 1797.

The outpouring of support for Snow Library was immediate after the fire. Donations of books and funds and offers of physical labor came in from all over the country. Within two years, a new library had been constructed.

Named for a man whose humble roots grew in Orleans soil, or rather "on a barren stretch of land on the outskirts of town," as he stated in his 1875 memoir, David Snow's hardworking and enterprising disposition led him from clam-shucking to carpentry to baking and finally to a Boston wharf-

Snow Library in 1937. *The William Brewster Nickerson Cape Cod History Archives, the Wilkens Library, Cape Cod Community College.*

front store selling flour, mackerel and alewives. In his twenties he discovered the world of books and began to realize what he'd missed by having to earn a living instead of getting an education, so he spent every bit of his spare time reading. Snow went on to build new ships and new wharves, becoming a financier and, after buying Constitution Wharf in Boston Harbor, a real estate mogul as well.

In 1876, the *Boston Journal* published his entire will, which included a sum of $5,000 for his hometown to build a library. Snow prophesied,

> *The legacy of the means of supplying a public library to Orleans will be productive of great good, if the people of that town will also learn everyday wisdom and practical prudence from the voice of their departed towns boy, who being dead yet speaketh.*

He certainly had a way with words. The original Snow Library stood on the southeast corner of Route 28 and Main Street for seventy-five years; the present library building was erected opposite the old site. After several renovations since 1954, there's a great art gallery, performance space and meeting rooms, along with lots of tables and chairs for working and reading.

After the original library burned down in 1952, this new version found a home on Main Street in Orleans. *Author's collection.*

The Marion Craine Room shows feature movies in "Snow Cinema" each Wednesday during the winter; there are also book discussion groups, story times for the little kids, art projects for older kids and a colorful monthly newsletter cleverly titled the *Snow Globe*. The Friends of the Snow Library raise funds for upgraded equipment and offer "Lifetime Learning" courses, book and author luncheons and many other programs.

In addition to sixty thousand books and other materials in its collection, the library owns more than seven hundred glass-plate negatives of the Orleans and Eastham area taken between 1887 and 1905 by H.K. Cummings.

Another Snow, a relative of David, was responsible for the town being named Orleans. Isaac Snow (1758–1855) fought in the Revolutionary War and was captured—twice—by the British. He escaped from an English prison ship, made his way to France and met Marquis de Lafayette and Count d'Estaing, who got him home to America aboard their fleet. Meanwhile, he had heard the stories about Louis Philippe Joseph, Duke of Orleans, France, a naval officer there who was fighting his own family in the cause of liberty. This impressed Isaac Snow, so when he returned to Cape Cod as a war hero, the legislature took his suggestion to name the town Orleans. It didn't hurt that the French had been supportive of America against the British during the war and that no one wanted to name the town for a place back in England at this point in history, so Orleans became the official name.

Snow Library is a busy place; programs held throughout the year total over 600, with annual transactions numbering almost 167,000. Plenty of everyday wisdom and practical prudence can be found here, and that would make its namesake benefactor proud.

PART IV

———— • ————

The Outer Cape

EASTHAM

EASTHAM PUBLIC LIBRARY
190 SAMOSET ROAD, EASTHAM, MA 02642
508-240-5950
WWW.EASTHAMLIBRARY.ORG

I have always imagined that Paradise will be a kind of a Library.
—Jorge Luis Borges (1899–1986, Argentine writer)

This one has undergone the most fantastic transformation of any library on the Cape. It also has a punny motto: "For Every Chapter of Your Life."

Eastham Library began life as many other Cape Cod libraries—as a few shelves inside the town's general store and post office. On land given by William Nickerson to the Village Improvement Society, the library got its own building on Samoset Road in 1898. In 1903, the VIS sold it to the town (for a dollar) and Robert C. Billings bequeathed a welcome $15,000. It's now listed on the National Register of Historic Places.

From the Ninth Report of the Free Public Library Commission, 1899:

> *The Public Library of Eastham was established in 1878 by vote and an appropriation of $100. At the same time gifts were received from Augustus Denton of Boston, $100; from the Ladies' Social Circle of Eastham, $100; and from the Ladies' Independent Social and Benevolent Association*

The 1897 Eastham Library was a big improvement on hardware store shelves of books. *Eastham Historical Society Archives.*

of Eastham, $116.11. An annual appropriation of $50 and the refunded dog tax, about $40, is now made by the town for the library. It is free to all inhabitants of Eastham and managed by three trustees chosen by the town. It had from its establishment occupied a room over the store of George H. Clark, loaned by him to the trustees, lighted and warmed and free of rent, but has recently been moved into a new building erected by the Village Improvement Society, and leased at a nominal rent to the town. Under authority of the Acts of 1892, this town, in 1893, was given $100 worth of books by the Free Public Library Commission. The library is open on Saturdays from 1 to 5 P.M. School teachers have the privilege of taking as many books as they desire, for use in the schoolroom and librarian and trustees offer all information and instruction possible to the town's people.

The small, boxy library served the town well for over one hundred years, but even with a few modest renovations here and there, the books were getting too numerous and therefore too squashed. The town studied, researched, compared and produced a most glorious plan: a truly grand renovation.

Carefully designed to honor rather than overwhelm the historic one-room library, the seventeen-thousand-square-foot addition was situated to the side and back of the original building. When construction began, the little library was plucked out of the way by a giant crane, set aside where it would stay out of mischief and eventually brought back to become the front of the new building, unharmed.

Soaring windows now lavish light on the red furniture in Eastham Public Library. Where the glass panes meet at the apex of a sharp triangle, a pair of binoculars and a bird book tempt visitors to look out over Depot Pond at Cape Cod wildlife. The views both inside and outside the library are spectacular.

Features include a reading garden, fireplace and community room as well as state-of-the-art green technologies to preserve the environment. The stunning design won one of six American Institute of Architects and

The spectacular contemporary design of Eastham Library incorporates a wall of windows overlooking Depot Pond. *Author's collection.*

American Library Association Library Building Awards in 2018. Patrons can't help exclaiming about the giant windows and wood vaulted ceilings. Eastham easily has the most exquisite library on the Cape. Others are cuter, quainter or have more old-fashioned character, but this one is just gorgeous.

In other news, only a creative and dedicated group like the Friends of the Eastham Library could imagine and implement a successful yearly festival around a vegetable so maligned as the lowly turnip—but they have.

It's hilariously ironic that thousands of eager fans flock to Eastham each November to celebrate a root that far fewer people in the whole world probably actually find tasty. But who can resist a turn at turnip bowling? Grownups walking about in white and lavender, dressed as turnips? Samples of every conceivable recipe using official grown-in-Eastham turnips? The event is free, with any proceeds benefitting the library. The profits are both money and joy.

32

WELLFLEET

WELLFLEET PUBLIC LIBRARY
55 WEST MAIN STREET, WELLFLEET, MA 02667
508-349-0310
WWW.WELLFLEETLIBRARY.ORG

With a library you are free, not confined by temporary political climates.
It is the most democratic of institutions because no one—but no one at all—can
tell you what to read and when and how.
—Doris Lessing (1919–2013, British-Zimbabwean novelist)

*I*t burned to the ground twice, but it rose again and again. Now, in a building where curtains and candles were once made, it feels that the Wellfleet Public Library was always meant to be here, so thoroughly at home it seems. There is whimsy in this place, along with serious studiousness. It's a pleasant contrast.

The current building was constructed in 1931 as Powdrell and Alexander Inc., which made curtains to be sold exclusively at Sears Roebuck. Later it was the home of the Colonial Candle Company. For a town with a year-round population of about 3,500, it is philosophically significant that there are close to 100,000 items in the library's collection; the attendance at various programs is high per capita as well. Almost 30,000 people attended 1,100 events in 2019. These statistics prove true its motto: "Illuminating the community from our location in a renovated candle factory."

Wellfleet Library moved all over town before finding its permanent home on West Main Street. *Author's collection.*

When Wellfleet was settled by Europeans in the 1650s, it was referred to as Billingsgate because of the enormous amounts of fish available in Cape Cod Bay. (Billingsgate was, and is, a neighborhood of London known for its fish market.) Officially part of Eastham after the land was "bought" from the local Native tribe, by 1763 this district of North Eastham had become Wellfleet, a name intended to either remind people of the famous Wallfleet oysters from Blackwater Bay in England or to fool them into thinking they actually were. They needn't have. Wellfleet and its unique oysters grew into their own success stories. Every year, the population sextuples in the summer, and this affects the library favorably.

For instance, there's a summer book sale by the Friends of the Wellfleet Library (to which many hundreds of people make an annual pilgrimage), along with art shows and the competition for the Chamber of Commerce

Guidebook cover art. The Friends fund museum passes for both on-Cape sites and those in the Boston area, lectures and presentations, concerts, dance and poetry events and online services like Kanopy film streaming.

The library began in 1873 as a small collection of books housed in the vestry of the First Congregational Church. In 1893, in response to the Massachusetts Library Act of 1890, the town received its one-hundred-dollar allotment for books and set up the Workers Circulating Library upstairs in the Wellfleet Savings Bank, on the corner of Bank Street and Commercial Street, with 1,827 books. It eventually moved to a building on Main Street; in 1909, the whole place, and all its books, by now numbering 2,500, went up in flames.

A few more moves around town led to the library finding a home on the upper floor of Town Hall—which also burned to the ground during a March blizzard in 1960. Wellfleet Library rose again, appealed for donations of books and began looking for a permanent site. It took twelve years, but by 1989 the candle factory on West Main Street was renovated and ready for its one hundred eager volunteers to move twenty-five thousand books into the new space, over five times larger than its Town Hall location.

Wellfleet Public Library had found its home.

33

TRURO

Truro Public Library
7 Standish Way, North Truro, MA 02652
Phone: 508-487-1125
www.TruroLibrary.org

Everything you need for better future and success has already been written. And guess what? All you have to do is go to the library.
—*Henri Frederic Amiel (1821–1881, Swiss moral philosopher, poet and critic)*

The air of friendliness here starts with subdued lighting and a smart use of space that fosters congeniality. Bookshelves are at interesting angles, and groups of chairs seem to be inviting readers to join them. A large multi-panel quilt depicting scenes around town has hung on the back wall of the main reading room since it was presented by the Friends of the Truro Public Library in 1999, when the library opened at this location next to the post office.

Everything is colorful and carefully placed, from the fun paper flowers to the old card catalogue now in service as an organizer of seeds (one drawer is marked squash to zucchini) for patrons to select.

For all the pleasantness, it's still a serious library. There are almost fifty thousand things to borrow: books, of course, but also e-books, audiobooks, e-audiobooks, downloadable videos, magazine subscriptions and e-subscriptions. Its Library of Things to take out includes a telescope from the Aldrich Astronomical Society of Paxton, Massachusetts.

A whimsical sculpture overlooks the circulation desk in Truro Public Library. *Author's collection.*

Like all Outer Cape towns, Truro is small in the winter and big in the summer, but year-rounders get plenty of attention from their library. Book clubs, story times, the immensely popular Truro Playgroup for infants and toddlers, a Lego Club and lectures "on everything from health to weather to economics to art" take place in this nice space, along with movies, game nights and music. There was even a Halloween party with a DJ and "Dancing in the Stacks." The Friends of the Truro Library provide financial support for programming and technology as well as the Winter Music Series, and they run Truro's only bookstore, Books Down Under (under the library, that is).

Genealogical researchers are offered many reference resources on old Truro families, such as Early Vital Records, local histories, cemetery indexing and Truro annual town reports from 1894 forward. That was also the year public library service was established at the town meeting; there were already three private lending libraries in town, but not one central library for all citizens, so within months a *public* library was created in Truro Center. In 1912, businessman Elisha Cobb gave the town a new Craftsman-style library in memory of his parents, naming it Cobb Memorial Library.

A decade later, the village of North Truro got its own public library, The Pilgrim Memorial Library, at the corner of Shore and Highland Roads, with funds raised by the "Pilgrim Pageant" in 1920. Though the three hundredth anniversary of the Pilgrims settling in Massachusetts was commemorated in hundreds of towns and cities that year, it had perhaps a bit more significance in Truro. The *Mayflower* passengers spent the second night of their arrival in the New World (new to them, not to the thousands of Native Americans already here) in East Harbor, Truro (or Payomet, as the Pamet tribe called the area). According to the 1622 journal of Englishman Edward Winslow, "There we saw a deer and found springs of fresh water, of which we were heartily glad, and set us down and drunk our first New England water with as much delight as ever we drank in all our lives."

The Pilgrim Memorial Library and Cobb Library consolidated in 1999 as Truro Public Library, and the Cobb building is now the Cobb Archive of Truro Historical Society, on the National Register of Historic Places.

Truro Public Library's logo states, "Books and More for Our Community," with a smiling frog, sitting on a bench, reading—that says it all.

34

PROVINCETOWN

PROVINCETOWN PUBLIC LIBRARY
356 COMMERCIAL STREET, PROVINCETOWN, MA 02657
508-487-7094
WWW.PROVINCETOWNLIBRARY.ORG

Bad libraries build collections, good libraries build services,
great libraries build communities.
—*R. David Lankes (professor and director of the School of Library &*
Information Science at the University of South Carolina)

Yes, there's a sixty-six-foot half-size model of a schooner in this library, and yes, its masts do poke through the ceiling more than twenty-five feet above the ship's deck, but Provincetown Library is a good deal more than theatrics—though the *Rose Dorothea is* pretty spectacular.

The building itself is enormous, with a one-hundred-foot steeple. Starting life in 1861 as the Center Methodist Episcopal Church, its 128 pews had seating for 900 people. The windows were made fifteen feet tall to illuminate church services during those pre-Edison days.

When the Methodist congregation sold the building in 1958, Walter P. Chrysler Jr. bought it and made it into an art museum, which lasted for twelve years; the problem was the bane of all of Provincetown's existence: parking. The town is full of charming-but-twisty narrow streets, houses whose façades sit within inches of the roads and so many visitors walking about almost year-round. There are several big parking lots, but they're a bit pricey and sometimes far away from Commercial Street, the main thoroughfare.

Does this discourage tourism? Not one bit. Provincetown is too special to let a shortage of parking deter visitors. However, objective reality intervenes on occasion, and if you really cannot find a place to leave your car, you can't visit a museum or library. So, the Chrysler Art Museum folded in 1970.

Another attempt to convert the church building into a center for the arts occurred in 1974, but it too was unsuccessful; by 1975, the Historic District Study Committee and the Provincetown Historical Association had the place certified on the National Register of Historic Places, which described it, in part, as a "fine example of Greek revival with English baroque elements. An important visual landmark from the sea and surrounding community."

The Massachusetts Historical Commission requires properties on the National Register of Historic Places to be held to an exceedingly high standard of renovations; it may be less expensive or more expedient to cut corners or forego strict adherence to historic details, but what would be lost is just too valuable. The former Methodist Church, then art museum, center for the arts and heritage museum needed to have its grand staircases restored and updated with proper railings, and its dramatic vaulted ceiling eventually had to be strengthened for those tall masts of the model *Rose Dorothea* schooner.

The new Provincetown Heritage Museum opened at 356 Commercial Street just in time for the American bicentennial on July 4, 1976. Francis "Flyer" Santos spent a decade creating a half-scale model of the original *Rose Dorothea*, a Grand Banks fishing schooner that won the Lipton Cup race during the 1907 Boston-Gloucester Fisherman's Race. Captain Santos was a custom boat designer and expert builder who owned Flyers Boat Yard in Provincetown for over seventy years; he lived to be one hundred, and his portrait hangs in the library. In 1950, he founded the West End Racing Club to "give kids an opportunity to learn how to sail and enrich their lives with nautical experience." He finished the highly detailed *Rose Dorothea* in 1988. It was one of the most popular exhibits in the museum through 2000.

However, when the need for a bigger public library coincided with waning Heritage Museum attendance, town officials began to consider transforming the huge old church into a space in which the old library, just a few blocks away at the corner of Freeman Street and Commercial Street, could move to and grow.

In a town full of attractions, Provincetown Public Library is a favorite of tourists as well as residents. *Charlene M. Hogan.*

The Provincetown Public Library opened its doors in 2005 to wild acclaim.

There was no question that the *Rose Dorothea* would stay in the building (only partly because it couldn't actually leave); it was, and is, a fascinating peek into the life of a fishing village. Then there are the truly inspired creative touches in the library, like custom-built bookcases embellished with mahogany armrests from pews found stacked in the church basement during an earlier renovation. Children's books are stored on blue shelves shaped like ocean waves, and the streetlamp lighting makes it feel like an actual wharf.

The new space has lots of natural light and pleasant pastel walls; the view out of the third-floor mezzanine is not to be missed, as all of Provincetown Harbor unfolds before you. The *Rose Dorothea* is in the center of the library's

A half-scale model of the *Rose Dorothea* schooner took ten years to build inside the library. *Susan Willis Davis.*

Children's Area, though you won't need a floor plan to find it.

The library has ongoing partnerships and collaborations with the town's schools and municipal departments, and there are amazingly well-attended annual events such as the Moby-Dick Marathon reading (now temporarily a virtual Moby-Dick Week instead) and the Provincetown Book Festival, two days of literary events for book lovers featuring more than a dozen diverse activities; in excess of six hundred attend each year. There's an extensive LGBTQ+ collection, not only of books but also information on legal rights, health, education and anti-bullying resources for schools.

"Crop Swap" is an innovative collaboration between the library, the Provincetown Health Department and the Soup Kitchen in Provincetown (SKIP). Those who have more fresh produce than they want can leave it in the dedicated refrigerator for those who need some.

The library hosts a Provincetown Community Support Liaison, offering residents free help:

> *To identify and address issues that affect your health, housing, and self-sufficiency; connect with other programs, agencies, and nonprofits to provide you with the most effective and beneficial resources and services; apply for fuel assistance, housing programs and funding, and other benefits; develop and manage a budget; connect with mental health and substance use services; and identify, set, and achieve goals to become more self-sufficient and thrive.*

Provincetown Library counted 180,000 visits in 2019; it has 71,000 items in its collection, and more than 5,000 people attend programs and events here in an average year.

It might be hard to find a parking spot sometimes, but it's well worth the effort.

BIBLIOGRAPHY

The American Stationer: A Journal Devoted to the Interests of the Stationery and Fancy Goods Trades 7, no. 1 (January 1879). Whole No. 184.

Cape Cod Magazine, August 1927.

A Historical Sketch of the Libraries of Cape Cod and Martha's Vineyard & Nantucket. N.p.: Cape Cod Library Club, 1952.

Ives, Josephine, and Sybille Colby. *A Beacon for Chatham.* Chatham, MA: Friends of the Eldredge Public Library, 1996.

Lovell, Russell A. *Sandwich: A Cape Cod Town.* Sandwich, MA, 1984.

Massachusetts Board of Library Commissioners Report. United States: n.p., 1899 and 1910.

New York Times. "Insanity Charged in Bourne Contest." May 24, 1923.

Other References

Falmouth Enterprise

National Register of Historic Places

Yarmouth Register

The websites for each library, each town report for 2019 and each town's historical society

ABOUT THE AUTHOR

Gerree Quinn Hogan's second-happiest place to be is in a library. She was a features writer for *Cape Cod Magazine* and the arts and entertainment editor for the *Falmouth Enterprise*. Hogan lives in Hyannis, Massachusetts, with her spouse and their two spoiled cats.